I0815406

FIGHTING *the* GOOD FIGHT
DEVOTIONAL FOR MEN

BOOKS BY TONY EVANS FROM BETHANY HOUSE PUBLISHERS

Kingdom Men Rising
Kingdom Men Rising Devotional
Kingdom Values
Kingdom Values Devotional
Kingdom Kindness
Kingdom Wisdom Devotional for Graduates
Fighting the Good Fight Devotional for Men

DAILY INSPIRATION TO STAND STRONG IN FAITH

FIGHTING *The* GOOD FIGHT

DEVOTIONAL FOR MEN

TONY EVANS

BETHANY HOUSE
a division of Baker Publishing Group
Minneapolis, Minnesota

Published by Bethany House Publishers
Minneapolis, Minnesota
BethanyHouse.com

Bethany House Publishers is a division of
Baker Publishing Group, Grand Rapids, Michigan

Printed in the United States of America

ISBN 9780764244902 (cloth)
ISBN 9781493451197 (ebook)

Library of Congress Cataloging-in-Publication Control Number: 2025007127

Devotions 141–170 are adapted from entries originally published in *Time to Get Serious: Daily Devotions to Keep You Closer to God* by Tony Evans, Crossway, 2007.

Baker Publishing Group publications use paper produced from sustainable forestry practices and postconsumer waste whenever possible.

25 26 27 28 29 30 31 7 6 5 4 3 2 1

THE BATTLE BEHIND THE SCENES

Did you know that a world you can't see may be having a huge impact on the one you can? Let me explain. Right now, you and I are in the middle of a cosmic conflict occurring in the invisible angelic realm. This battle is being fleshed out and worked out in the very visible physical realm in which we live.

Perhaps you are an emotional casualty of this warfare, and this is evidenced by discouragement, depression, or despair. Or perhaps you have been affected in your marriage or relationships by this conflict. It is even possible that your financial situation is directly related to losing the ongoing battles in this warfare, and you thought it simply was related to credit card use or otherwise piling up debt. There is no end to the scope of this battle because Satan's goal is to sideline you from living as an active participant in God's kingdom army. The problem is that most of us forget to look at the true source behind the issues we face. As a result, we end up fighting the wrong enemy. The enemy is the devil and his minions. Once you recognize that our battle is not against flesh and blood but is in the spiritual realm, you are better equipped to wage spiritual warfare well and successfully.

EPHESIANS 6:12 *For our struggle is not against flesh and blood, but against the rulers, against the powers, against the world forces of this darkness, against the spiritual forces of wickedness in the heavenly places.*

—2—

PEOPLE AREN'T YOUR PROBLEM

If you feel like somebody's out to get you, you are right. But it's probably not who you think it is.

The apostle Paul says you are making a huge mistake if you think people are the root of your problem. He tells us in Ephesians 6:12 that we wrestle not against "flesh and blood," which refers to people. So, as bad as people are, they are merely the conduits of another battle. But Satan has been successful in getting us to fight people rather than the enemy causing the people to be the way that they are.

All of us have been in situations where we've tried to change people who are not behaving well or are not treating us as we'd prefer. Yet, until you and I understand that what happens to us through the actions of others has at its core something much bigger than those people, we will remain in a state of deception. This is exactly where Satan wants us to remain. So if you are ready to treat the disease instead of just the symptoms, level up your skills in spiritual warfare. Learn how to get to the root of people problems—as well as even more serious concerns, such as substance abuse and sexual, emotional, or relational issues—by studying and applying principles for waging spiritual warfare with excellence.

ROMANS 12:18 *If possible, so far as it depends on you, be at peace with all men.*

—3—

TWO WORLDVIEWS

Do you ever catch yourself thinking that things "just happen" in your life? The Bible has an important perspective on this, and I have come to believe that nothing happens without a reason. God either allowed it to happen or intended it to happen. This is because everything in the physical realm in which we live is influenced, or provoked, by the spiritual realm. There is nothing your five senses partake of that is not influenced by what your five senses do not perceive.

Daniel 4:26 summarizes how heaven rules over what takes place on earth: "Your kingdom will be assured to you after you recognize that it is heaven that rules." Essentially, everything that takes place on earth is precipitated by something that took place in heaven.

Until you and I can address the spiritual causes of the issues we face in our lives, we will never fix them. This reality should help frame our worldview. Now, there really are only two worldviews: There is the naturalistic worldview that says mankind, by his own reason, can figure out how the world works. On the other side is the spiritual worldview, which reflects an understanding and acknowledgment that heaven rules over all. To embrace this worldview, you must understand its essence, which is that the battle you and I are engaged in is ultimately a spiritual one.

MATTHEW 6:10 *Your kingdom come. Your will be done, on earth as it is in heaven.*

If you want to attack your problems at the root, you might have to dig deeper than you expected.

—4—

ROOT PROBLEMS

If you want to attack your problems at the root, you might have to dig deeper than you expected. The battle in which you and I are engaged is essentially spiritual. However, even though it is spiritual in its cause, it is physical in its effect.

Many of you reading this devotional find your personal life is a disaster. And that doesn't mean you're out there doing something terrible. It could be that you have uncontrolled anger or an inability to restrain your emotions. In fact, many of us are suffering today because of unresolved anger from our past. Unfortunately, we have been lulled into thinking that someone just did us wrong, but really it was Satan who sought to contrive a situation so he could get hold of our emotions. When Satan gets a grip on your emotions, he destroys your ability to function properly.

Too many men struggle with emotional disconnection in their marriages because their feelings have been sidelined due to past sin—whether they committed the sin themselves or whether something was done to them. The key to reclaiming emotional freedom and control lies in learning how to tell when your problems are merely symptoms of the invisible spiritual battle going on around you, then discovering the tactics and approaches to winning those specific battles once and for all.

EPHESIANS 6:8 *Knowing that whatever good thing each one does, this he will receive back from the Lord, whether slave or free.*

— 5 —

WHERE THE BLESSINGS ARE

Victory comes in discovering how to fight what you cannot see. Ephesians 1:3 provides insight: "Blessed be the God and Father of our Lord Jesus Christ, who has blessed us with every spiritual blessing in the heavenly places in Christ."

The first important thing to notice in this verse is that it tells us where God the Father resides: in heavenly places. While most of us already know that to be true, the next part of the verse is more revealing. In it we learn that our blessings also reside in heavenly places. The meaning of this is profound. If you are in the midst of a spiritual war and need spiritual blessings in order to win it but you don't know how to access those blessings in heavenly places, you will continue to lose in the spiritual warfare on earth.

Ephesians 2:6 shows us how to access these blessings by revealing where we ourselves are actually residing. It says, "and raised us up with Him, and seated us with Him in the heavenly places in Christ Jesus." When you accepted Jesus Christ as your Savior, you were transported to another realm. Even though your physical body is here, your spiritual self, which controls your body, operates from heavenly places. Reorient your thinking to understand (A) where you are spiritually, (B) what you can gain from being there, and (C) what benefits flow from Who you know.

EPHESIANS 2:6 *And raised us up with Him, and seated us with Him in the heavenly places in Christ Jesus.*

—6—

IT TAKES AN ANGEL

Satan is a powerful enemy, one you don't have the power to beat on your own. But that's why the Lord levels the playing field—and then some. We gain insight into this by reading Ephesians 3:10, which says, "so that the manifold wisdom of God might now be made known through the church to the rulers and the authorities in the heavenly places." What's important to note is that the terms *rulers* and *authorities* in this passage refer to the angels. It is critical to understand this because it takes an angel to defeat an angel.

If you are facing angelic problems in your life (remember, Satan is a fallen angel), then you need an angelic solution.

Most of us have very little consciousness of angels because they are not part of our physical experience. But the battle taking place all around us—and even within us—involves a whole group of angels. The Bible calls God the "Lord of Hosts," and what that title means is that God, in a military sense, is in charge of an angelic corps whose job involves strategizing against and defeating the demons who seek to defeat you.

You do not have enough power or strength to defeat demons. But God does. Asking God to send angels to neutralize the demons attacking you is a wise use of spiritual weaponry.

EPHESIANS 3:10 *So that the manifold wisdom of God might now be made known through the church to the rulers and the authorities in the heavenly places.*

7

IT'S ABOUT THE GLORY

You can't win a spiritual battle with just physical common sense or strategy. You must wage a spiritual battle with spiritual sense and truth. In Revelation 12 we read about a day when war will break out in a visible form like we've never seen before. Spiritual war will come to earth. Revelation 12:7–9 says,

> And there was war in heaven, Michael and his angels waging war with the dragon. The dragon and his angels waged war, and they were not strong enough, and there was no longer a place found for them in heaven. And the great dragon was thrown down, the serpent of old who is called the devil and Satan, who deceives the whole world; he was thrown down to the earth, and his angels were thrown down with him.

There exist two squads: Michael and the good angels on one side, Satan and the bad angels on the other. We are in an angelic conflict started through rebellion, and Satan is attempting to deceive the world into glorifying him. This war boils down to who gets the glory. When you know the goal of a battle, you know how to approach it. That's why Paul reminds us that whatever we do, we are to do it all to the glory of God (1 Corinthians 10:31). One way to keep yourself from ending up as a casualty of this conflict is to always seek God's glory first.

1 CORINTHIANS 10:31 *Whether, then, you eat or drink or whatever you do, do all to the glory of God.*

—8—

SATAN'S STRATEGY

In a battle, it's always important to figure out what your enemy is trying to do before he does it. That's why you need to know Satan's strategy, or he can easily take advantage of you. Second Corinthians 2:11 emphasizes this, "so that no advantage would be taken of us by Satan, for we are not ignorant of his schemes."

Satan has a plan, a scheme. Just as he deceived Eve, and then Adam, in the garden, he has a plan of deception targeted at you and those you love. Satan is very crafty. Paul warns in 2 Corinthians 11:3, "I am afraid that, as the serpent deceived Eve by his craftiness, your minds will be led astray from the simplicity and purity of devotion to Christ."

Satan's tactic is deception. If you want to understand Satan and what he's trying to do in your life, start by realizing that he's trying to trick you. He's good at making you think things that simply are not true. What's more, he sometimes offers you a good time while doing it. But anybody who comes to Jesus Christ can be delivered from the domain of the devil and his deception. It takes a concentrated focus on the truth of God's Word along with the abiding presence of Jesus in your life. This is one way to stay on top of Satan's schemes so you are not a victim to his deceiving ways.

2 CORINTHIANS 2:11 *So that no advantage would be taken of us by Satan, for we are not ignorant of his schemes.*

—9—

SOLDIERS OR CIVILIANS

If you're not seeing victory in spiritual warfare, maybe you are ill-equipped for the battle. Acts 26:18 says, in summary, that anybody who comes to Jesus Christ is delivered from the domain of the devil. God has set you free: "to open their eyes so that they may turn from darkness to light and from the dominion of Satan to God, that they may receive forgiveness of sins and an inheritance among those who have been sanctified by faith in Me."

The problem is that it's possible to be set free yet still feel chained. Too many men today have become accustomed to living in bondage. But he whom the Son sets free is free indeed (John 8:36). This freedom is realized through trusting God to fight the battles for you. When God fights spiritual battles on your behalf, you will win; but when you show up to do battle yourself, you will be defeated.

The government of a nation at war focuses on caring for soldiers, not civilians. Spiritual warfare is no different. Yet too many Christians are living as civilians rather than as soldiers in this war. To war God's way, you'll need to enlist in His spiritual army and follow His commands. Then you can expect Him to equip you for the battle at hand.

ACTS 26:18 *To open their eyes so that they may turn from darkness to light and from the dominion of Satan to God, that they may receive forgiveness of sins and an inheritance among those who have been sanctified by faith in Me.*

—10—

DEVILISH THINKING

What earned Satan a one-way trip to the lake of fire? It was the same sin that brings down many of us: pride. God created Satan perfect. He had no flaws. In fact, Satan held a high position in God's angelic realm. The problem came when he looked in the mirror one day and began admiring himself. He began to take stock of all he had been given by God: wisdom, glory, beauty, power, and wit. Satan added up his personal assets and determined he could make it on his own.

Are there any Lucifers reading this devotional right now? If you have been a recipient of God's blessings, whether in your skills, gifts, finances, relationships, or more—you might be tempted to believe Lucifer's lie. You might be tempted to believe you don't need God to make it in this life. The Bible calls people who think like that the children of the devil (John 8:44). One of the most dangerous positions spiritually is to be successful in our physical, temporal world. It is easy to forget that it is God who gave you the power to acquire the wealth and success you have. That's why the greatest sin in the Bible, as well as the primary method for spiritual defeat, is pride

DEUTERONOMY 8:18 *But you shall remember the Lord your God, for it is He who is giving you power to make wealth, that He may confirm His covenant which He swore to your fathers, as it is this day.*

—11—

ROYALLY BEATEN

When Satan and his fellow angels rebelled, they were thrown out of heaven. But there's more to the story. We see in Genesis 1 that when God created the earth, it was at first formless and void. Darkness covered the surface of it. The earth then wasn't a luxurious location filled with potential as we see today.

It wasn't until God made the light that the darkness was driven away to be contained within limits. God continued the steps of His creation, including the addition of trees and vegetation, and life could be sustained. God did this to provide a place for humanity to live. He chose to create people lesser than the angels to demonstrate to the angels that a lesser creature could trust God and glorify Him.

As humanity began to occupy the land and God provided the resources for it to be developed, Satan continued to seek to destroy God's creation. In short, Satan seeks to pervert the creative gifts God gave humanity for his own ends of emptiness and waste, the state of the earth before God's creation. Understanding this helps you navigate your choices in life. Any choice you make that brings about destruction or darkness—in your own life, in others' lives, as well as in the earth—is a choice Satan desires you to make. Align your decisions with God's divine will and you will defeat Satan in spiritual war.

GENESIS 1:3 *Then God said, "Let there be light"; and there was light.*

—12—

ADAM AND SATAN

When God created humanity, He paralleled the situation of Lucifer: Lucifer was created a perfect being with free will, and so was Adam.

Adam could eat freely of all the trees in the garden except one. God did not have an angel guard the tree; He just told Adam not to eat from it.

In addition to the ability to choose, there are other similarities between Lucifer and Adam. Adam's homestead was called Eden, and Ezekiel 28 says Lucifer's homestead was called Eden. Adam was to oversee all of God's creation. Lucifer was to oversee all of God's angelic creation. Adam and Eve walked with God in the garden. Lucifer functioned in close proximity to God before his fall from heaven.

With all these similarities, why did God take a chance on creating humanity? Because God wanted to show that He could create a lesser being who could choose what is right. Yes, Adam (and Eve) made poor choices. We all make wrong choices. But God is looking for followers who will repent and return to Him when they do. That is the difference between living for God and living for yourself, which is the way of the devil.

EZEKIEL 28:13 *You were in Eden, the garden of God; every precious stone was your covering: the ruby, the topaz and the diamond; the beryl, the onyx and the jasper; the lapis lazuli, the turquoise and the emerald; and the gold, the workmanship of your settings and sockets, was in you. On the day that you were created they were prepared.*

— 13 —

WHY GOD ALLOWS WARFARE

One of the most common questions about spiritual warfare is, Why does God allow it? It's not for lack of power to stop it. No, through this angelic conflict, God wants all of us to see that He is a holy and perfect God, worthy of honor. He wants us to see His wisdom as well. Ephesians 3:10 says that God desires to make His manifold wisdom known to all. God also wants to demonstrate His power. You won't know how powerful He is until there's opposition. The Israelites saw God's power when He set them free from the bondage of Pharaoh. Moses got to see God's power when God parted the Red Sea. We get to see God's power when we take our spiritual battles to Him in prayer, follow His lead, and witness His seeing us through.

God also allows spiritual warfare for reasons we can't begin to understand. We read in Isaiah that not everything He does is for us to scrutinize and comprehend. That's why faith is so important.

Trusting that God has a plan is part of the plan. Allow God to be God without having to define and dissect all that He does. In doing so, you demonstrate faith in the One who knows all and rules over all, and you bring Him glory.

ISAIAH 55:9 *For as the heavens are higher than the earth, so are My ways higher than your ways and My thoughts than your thoughts.*

—14—

FOCUS ON THE YES

Magicians use misdirection to shift your focus from where the trick is being done. Satan uses the same technique when he tempts us. But there is a way to see beyond the sleight of hand Satan so craftily employs, and it involves opening your eyes to God's blessings in your life.

When God commanded Adam not to eat from the Tree of Knowledge of Good and Evil, He didn't leave Adam empty-handed. He had given Adam a garden full of trees to enjoy. Had Adam focused on all the yeses from God, he would not have sinned. Adam's decision to disobey God revealed a heart that did not believe God. He tested God and paid for his disbelief for the rest of his life.

Many parents see this at Christmas. Even though you might have gotten your child nine presents, he or she is looking for the tenth. The devil uses greed to cause you to miss out on the goodness of God. Satan cleverly hides what God has blessed you with so you will look only at the tree God told you not to touch. Opening your spiritual eyes so you are grateful for all you do have enables you to find the strength to resist temptation. Experiencing victory in spiritual warfare requires shifting your gaze from Satan's sleight of hand to God's bountiful provisions, responding with a heart of thanksgiving.

GENESIS 2:17 *But from the tree of the knowledge of good and evil you shall not eat, for in the day that you eat from it you will surely die.*

15

THE SECOND ADAM

If spiritual warfare were a chess game, Jesus Christ would be God's checkmate move. Scripture tells us why: "Now the promises were spoken to Abraham and to his seed. He does not say, 'And to seeds,' as referring to many, but rather to one, 'And to your seed,' that is, Christ" (Galatians 3:16). And, "But when the fullness of the time came, God sent forth His Son, born of a woman, born under the Law" (Galatians 4:4).

We can see that these verses, and the whole biblical story, point to Jesus. This is because every man sins. To believe that there are men, even in ministry positions, who do not or have not sinned, is to not understand the Bible. The reason Jesus came is because we all are in need of a Savior. Jesus is our covering. He is our salvation. It is His death, burial, and resurrection that give us eternal life. If you know Jesus Christ as your Savior, you know how to make a checkmate move on the devil. Christ's blood is your checkmate move on Satan.

Humility is the first step to an abiding relationship with Jesus Christ. When you are humble, you activate the Holy Spirit's power in your life to work on your behalf. Acknowledging your sinfulness to yourself and to God unleashes this flow of humility, strengthening you in your ability to overcome and gain victory in spiritual battles.

GALATIANS 4: *So that He might redeem those who were under the Law, that we might receive the adoption as sons.*

16

IT'S NOT A PARADE

Far too many of us gather on Sunday for church with expectations rooted not in Scripture but in cultural norms. We come to experience an event rather than to find out how to go to war. We come to be entertained, to network, or to check off a list. But the reason we should come to church is to get equipped in the Word of God, so we can more successfully wage our spiritual battles.

So because we have lost the true reason for Sunday gatherings, we wind up with many casualties on the battlefield. God isn't looking for part-time saints or weekend visitations. He wants you to live as a committed follower of Christ, always ready to battle spiritually.

We have too many walking wounded in our sanctuaries today. These are men who have been caught in the cross fire of the angelic conflict. The battle is upon us, whether we want it or not. Satan has taken the aggressor's role. You are a target. The Bible reveals that the whole world lies in the hands of the evil one. It was handed over as men joined Satan in his rebellion against God. But when you came to Jesus Christ, you were born into another world. You were born again into the family of God, and now you are fighting for victory on God's kingdom team.

EPHESIANS 6:19 *And pray on my behalf, that utterance may be given to me in the opening of my mouth, to make known with boldness the mystery of the gospel.*

— 17 —

THE DEVILISH AGENDA

The Bible tells us that Satan's fighting a war he can't possibly win. That truth raises a question I'm sure we all have considered at some point: Why does Satan keep fighting? He fights because he has an agenda. Satan's agenda is to bring the world under his control and make Christians ineffective at bringing others out of the war zone. Satan seeks to stop us from leading others to victory. He's after the casualties.

To rack up those casualties, Satan attacks in a number of ways. And no matter who you are or what your status, Satan wants to overthrow you or neutralize you for God's kingdom.

When you look closely at Christians today, you find many who are in the POW camps. Satan has overthrown them in the area of drugs, and they are held hostage. He has overthrown them in the area of alcohol, and they are held hostage. He has overthrown them in the area of discouragement and depression, and they are prisoners of war. He has overthrown them in a variety of areas—in a variety of ways. He doesn't care *how* he ensnares believers, only *that* he ensnares believers, causing them to be prisoners of him rather than servants of God. That's why you must gain wisdom about how to cease being a victim of the spiritual battle raging all around you.

1 PETER 5:8 *Be of sober spirit, be on the alert. Your adversary, the devil, prowls around like a roaring lion, seeking someone to devour.*

—18—

THE WAR OF THE SEEDS

Satan isn't just after *you*. He is after everyone within your sphere of influence, including your kids. Why is the family so important to Satan? Because the ultimate battle will be waged by the seed. It will be waged by the offspring. Thus, Satan wants to destroy your family not only because he wants you, but because he wants the next generation.

If Satan can get the next generation under his control or within his grip before you have a chance to mold, shape, steer, direct, or guide them, he will have nearly certain influence over them and their seed to come. If Satan can get them because of a messed-up home, he not only now has your home, he has their home, more than likely. It then becomes a generational problem because the battle is being waged by the seed.

The tragedy today is that Christians are still fighting flesh and blood rather than recognizing they are fighting principalities and powers and world forces. Strategies and battle plans against flesh and blood do not defeat principalities and powers in the spiritual realm. As a result, Satan's forces wind up devastating these Christians.

That's why you've got to fight for your family. Whoever controls the family controls the future.

NEHEMIAH 4:14 *When I saw their fear, I rose and spoke to the nobles, the officials and the rest of the people: "Do not be afraid of them; remember the Lord who is great and awesome, and fight for your brothers, your sons, your daughters, your wives and your houses."*

19

SPOTTING SATAN IN THE SANCTUARY

The very place Christians should go to learn how to beat Satan in spiritual war often becomes the very place where Satan beats them: the church. Satan knows how important the church is, so he attacks it regularly by promoting disunity, division, discrimination, culturism, and more. Satan wants to split up the family of God because Satan understands something many Christians don't: God works in a context of unity.

There must be harmony to see the full expression of the power of God. Thus, if Satan can split the church up through difficulties and divisions, the body of Christ becomes an easy target.

We all share a common battle against a common enemy. One of the reasons our communities are in disarray is because churches have been emphasizing membership over fellowship and discipleship. Fellowship means that if you belong to Jesus Christ, even though we don't all dot our i's and cross our t's alike, we're still spelling the same name: *Jesus Christ*. It is incumbent on us to recognize that our fellowship is in Christ and our discipleship should follow suit. As you wage spiritual warfare, be an influence of positive reinforcement for your church, encouraging members to focus on what matters most, and not on mere numbers.

1 TIMOTHY 3:15 *But in case I am delayed, I write so that you will know how one ought to conduct himself in the household of God, which is the church of the living God, the pillar and support of the truth.*

—20—

SATAN AND THE NATIONS

Satan is behind princes. He's behind kings. He sits back there, provoking, empowering, and enabling them to destroy whole nations and groups of people. When you understand that this is his plan, you understand we are in a spiritual battle. He wants to kill or imprison you as an individual as well as your family.

Transforming a nation for God involves more than who you elect. It has to do with how the body of Christ wages spiritual warfare in their own lives. If Satan can defeat each of us individually, he will remove our influence on our nation, whether that influence comes through prayer or activities.

Satan wants to disable each of us from leaving a lasting influence of goodness and grace upon the societies we live in. He wants to get us so caught up in our own dramas and our own issues and our own strongholds that we no longer have time to pray for the leaders in our land or seek what is good for society.

It's difficult for prisoners of war to defend or strengthen their nation. Thus, if you want to make a positive contribution to the society at large, you need to focus on your own spiritual warfare and become successful against the enemy's schemes.

EPHESIANS 2:2 *In which you formerly walked according to the course of this world, according to the prince of the power of the air, of the spirit that is now working in the sons of disobedience.*

—21—

IT'S ALL IN YOUR HEAD

People write off the idea of spiritual warfare by saying, "It's all in your head." And they might be right, to an extent. For example, when you wrestle with something day in and day out, week in and week out, it becomes the central thought in your head. It dominates your focus and influences your emotions. In fact, the source of many spiritual battles finds its root in your mind. And until you fix your mind and your thoughts, you will not solve the problems showing up in the rest of your life.

Second Corinthians 10:5 says, "We are destroying speculations and every lofty thing raised up against the knowledge of God, and we are taking every thought captive to the obedience of Christ."

Spiritual warfare has to do with the knowledge of God as well as taking every thought captive. Speculations have to do with the untruths that Satan seeks to entrap your thoughts with, and the location of these speculations is the mind. So in order for you to discover freedom from captivity in this spiritual battle, you must discover how to think anew. The battle takes place in your thoughts. Align your thoughts with the truth of God's Word, and you will be on your way to victory.

2 CORINTHIANS 10:4 *For the weapons of our warfare are not of the flesh, but divinely powerful for the destruction of fortresses.*

—22—

DEVILISH MIND GAMES

If you think your situation is hopeless, the problem might not be the situation. The problem might be your thinking. One of Satan's top moves is to influence you to adopt his thinking about whatever you are facing, rather than God's. If Satan can get you to think the way he wants you to think, he's won the battle. Satan seeks to set up strongholds, or walls, in your mind—walls to keep the truth from penetrating your thoughts. These are referred to as "fortresses" in 2 Corinthians 10:4, where it says, "For the weapons of our warfare are not of the flesh, but divinely powerful for the destruction of fortresses."

To engage in spiritual warfare is to tear down these walls so that the truth of God's Word can flow freely. Fortresses set up by Satan result in hopelessness and despair, leaving you despondent when you think there is no way to overcome your financial strains, relational stress, or career difficulties. But with God, there is always hope. He either grants the way through it or He gives you peace in it. Satan doesn't want you to know that, so he seeks to erect fortresses of falsehoods.

One way to live in victory over the spiritual struggles you face each day is to keep your mind focused on Christ and the Word of God. When you do that, you can tear down the walls Satan hopes to use to trap you.

2 CORINTHIANS 10:3 *For though we walk in the flesh, we do not war according to the flesh.*

—23—

THE AUTHORITY TO WIN

Satan is a defeated enemy but that doesn't mean he lacks power. He is powerful and dangerous, and that's why it takes spiritual authority to beat him. You can never overpower Satan, but you can defeat him based on the authority of Jesus Christ.

Satan wants you to think you do have the ability to overpower him so that when you try to fight him in your own strength, you'll quickly lose. As he continues to win battle after battle in that way, you'll start to believe you can never defeat him. That's when he has you right where he wants you.

The way to defeat Satan is to access spiritual authority through your ability to see Jesus and to tap into *His* overarching authority. Jesus has already won the battle for you. But if you can't see Him or if you don't know this, you will try to win on your own and you will lose every time.

Seeing Jesus comes through spending time with Him. We call that "abiding," which is just a nice way of describing what it's like to hang out with someone. Hanging out with Jesus on a regular basis enables you to see Him and hear Him during those times when you need Him most—times of spiritual warfare.

JOHN 15:5 *I am the vine, you are the branches; he who abides in Me and I in him, he bears much fruit, for apart from Me you can do nothing.*

—24—

BETWEEN THE CRUCIFIXION AND RESURRECTION

The Easter story talks about Jesus' crucifixion and resurrection. But what happened between those events is also critically important.

Between the crucifixion and the resurrection, God not only forgave our sins, but He also got Satan off our backs. So God sent Jesus to visit Hades: "When He ascended on high, He led captive a host of captives, and He gave gifts to men" (Ephesians 4:8). Jesus Christ went down to where the captives were and let them know He had paid the full price for their release. He set them free.

One way to consider this is that Jesus went to the abyss where Satan and his demons were incarcerated and holding others captive, and Jesus proclaimed victory. Satan hadn't counted on the death of Jesus Christ satisfying the justice of God as a full payment for sins. Satan knew about God's love and His wrath, but he hadn't known about the grace of God. God's grace allowed for Jesus to satisfy God's wrath so He could express His love without compromising His nature. It was the unveiling of the all-powerful grace of God, which is available to you today as you wage spiritual warfare.

EPHESIANS 4:7 *But to each one of us grace was given according to the measure of Christ's gift.*

—25—

THE TOOTHLESS LION

Satan didn't disappear when Jesus rose from the dead. Satan is still at large, still fighting. But we read in Colossians 2 that when Christ was resurrected, He disarmed Satan and took his weapons away. Verses 14–15 say that He "canceled out the certificate of debt consisting of decrees against us, which was hostile to us; and He has taken it out of the way, having nailed it to the cross. When He had disarmed the rulers and authorities, He made a public display of them, having triumphed over them through Him."

Not only was your sin paid in full on the cross, but Jesus also took away Satan's weapons. Jesus entered Satan's house of death and beat him at his own game, releasing those trapped there, the first to be redeemed. As Galatians 3:13 says, "Christ redeemed us from the curse of the Law, having become a curse for us—for it is written, 'CURSED IS EVERYONE WHO HANGS ON A TREE.'" Christ redeemed each of us from the curse of the Law, taking the curse upon himself. With that, He de-toothed the lion that seeks to devour you. If you are going to be victorious over Satan in the angelic conflict— though he still intimidates you and makes it seem as though the lions under his control have teeth—you must understand and remember your position in Jesus Christ and what Jesus accomplished on the cross.

COLOSSIANS 2:10 *And in Him you have been made complete, and He is the head over all rule and authority.*

—26—

ONE LAST MOVE

A story is told of a famous chess champion who was on vacation in Europe. He came to an art gallery and there was a painting of a chess game in progress. On one side of the chessboard was the devil, laughing and full of hilarity. On the other side of the chessboard was a young man who appeared to be distressed, hopeless.

Then the chess champion read the title above the painting: *The Chess Players*, also known as *Checkmate*. It appeared that the devil was about to make the final move to win this young man's soul. Yet, after a number of hours staring at the painting, the chess champion began to smile.

Addressing the young man in the picture, he said, "Mister, I sure wish you could hear me now, because I've got good news. It only looks like the devil is winning. But there is still one move left on the board, and you get to make it."

A lot of us have been duped into thinking the devil is winning—or even has won. We think he is the final decision-maker about our joy, happiness, well-being, spirituality, and all the other elements that make life work. But Jesus Christ has good news for you. The devil doesn't get the last move. You do. And in Christ, that move can be a move of victory.

COLOSSIANS 2:6 *Therefore as you have received Christ Jesus the Lord, so walk in Him.*

—27—

THE ROOT OF OUR PROBLEMS

In football, coaches watch the film of the other team to find their weaknesses. They then know how best to play against the opposing team. Satan is as smart, or smarter, than any football coach. He knows to watch you to observe and uncover your weaknesses too. In fact, believers have demons assigned to them. The demons' job is to make hell break loose in your life. The demonic realm knows your weak spots and what buttons to push. The demons know what happened when you were a child that messed up your thinking or lowered your self-esteem. They know about the sin patterns that have developed during your life that invite their demonic presence.

These principalities and powers in the spiritual realm do all they can to take advantage of your weak points. The physical world manifests what is happening in the spiritual world. Physical solutions can't fix the physical problems if the problems originated in the spiritual realm. You'll never find the cure if you don't first identify the cause. Shift your focus from the players on the field to the coaches in the boxes—the demons who are studying your film and seeking to exploit you. When you do that, you will know how important it is to stay right with God and use the power of Christ to defeat Satan in his deceptive strategies.

EPHESIANS 6:11 *Put on the full armor of God, so that you will be able to stand firm against the schemes of the devil.*

—28—

SATAN'S SCARY PITCHFORK

The devil and demons don't want you to know their methodology or their schemes. Because if you ever figure them out, you can overcome them. Just like a football team could easily beat an opponent if they got hold of their playbook, you could have the upper hand on the evil one if you got his playbook. That's why Satan aims to keep you looking at the physical realm as the source of your struggles. He doesn't want you to understand where the shots and the plays really are being called.

The devil wants you to think of him as a scary thing with a pitchfork and a red jumpsuit, but his schemes are much more subtle than that. If all you are looking for are witches and a forked tail, you might stop being watchful when you don't see them. You might end up not taking Satan seriously. His one overarching principle is to deceive, trick, and bamboozle you by showing up disguised as something good. A red jumpsuit and pitchfork are not going to trick you because they are what you are looking for. You are only deceived when Satan shows up in unexpected ways.

Yet, as long as you are under the protective covering of God, Satan can't get you. Your main focus ought to be on remaining underneath the covering of the blood of the Lord Jesus Christ and to ask the Spirit to open your eyes to the devil's schemes.

2 CORINTHIANS 11:14 *No wonder, for even Satan disguises himself as an angel of light.*

—29—

PRAIRIE FIRE

When you feel like you can't outrun your problems, the best advice might be to stop trying. Sometimes we try so hard to overcome the spiritual battles we are facing that we wear ourselves out. What's worse, often we even blame God when all our own attempts fall flat.

A hundred or so years ago, a father and son were trying to outrun a prairie fire in a wagon. They were going very fast, but the fire was moving faster; soon they would be consumed.

The father turned the wagon around and went to a spot that had already burned. The father and son jumped out and he told his son to stay there with him. The son argued because the fire was coming at them. But the father explained the need to stay within the safety of the burned-out area because the ground was already scorched and the fire would have nothing to catch on, so it would pass them by. That wisdom spared father and son.

Satan wants you to step out of the safe zone, where Jesus was already burned when He died on the cross. There is complete safety and security in Him. Jesus was crucified for all sin—yours included—and the resurrection has occurred. If you will stand firm on the cross of Jesus Christ, you will be safe from Satan's darts of fire. You are safe in Christ.

JOHN 3:16 *For God so loved the world, that He gave His only begotten Son, that whoever believes in Him shall not perish, but have eternal life.*

—30—

DIGITAL SPIRITUALITY

When digital streaming replaced analog transmitters, it was bad news for people who didn't upgrade their sets. Unfortunately, many believers have trouble "tuning in" to God for the same reason. They are too tied to the analogue, which can be compared to man's worldview and opinion. If you only go to social media, news media, and friends to get insight into how you should think or approach issues, you will miss out on God's supply of information and wisdom.

God will not force-feed you His Word, or strong-arm you into a close relationship with Him. God has given you the freedom to choose. You get to choose whether you make the world's perspective preeminent in your life or God's perspective.

When you spend hours a day scrolling online, you are inputting the world's perspective. This only strengthens Satan's ability to construct strongholds and fortresses of deception. It may feel innocent to you to simply scroll through information feeds, but over time it builds up to create clutter in your thoughts. God wants you to focus your thoughts on Him and His Word. This is done by cutting off the analogue connection and seeking Him through a deep, abiding, high-definition connection directly through prayer and His Word.

JOSHUA 1:8 *This book of the law shall not depart from your mouth, but you shall meditate on it day and night, so that you may be careful to do according to all that is written in it; for then you will make your way prosperous, and then you will have success.*

—31—

ARMED FOR SUCCESS

As we've discussed throughout this devotional, the problems and pain you experience in the earthly realm are the result of conflicts going on in the spiritual realm. So how can you defend yourself against attacks you can't see? It starts by opening your eyes to the spiritual realm. You need to learn to operate in the spiritual as easily and naturally as you do in the physical realm.

The Bible tells us in Romans 16:20 that God will soon crush Satan underneath our feet. That means the victory is promised as yours. You are not fighting *for* victory—you are fighting *from* victory. To live in the truth of that promised reality, you need to put on the full armor of God every day. When you wear the armor of God, you are dressed for success.

But let's get this straight—it's not *your* armor. It is God's armor. When you access the full armor available to you from God, you'll be able to handle anything Satan throws at you. You'll be able to handle your temper, your addictions, and your temptations. I'm not saying you won't be tempted, but you will be able to overcome it. Or, if you have given in to temptation, you will find the strength and conviction to stop what you are doing and repent. Satan will no longer be the dictator over what you do with your life.

EPHESIANS 6:13 *Therefore, take up the full armor of God, so that you will be able to resist in the evil day, and having done everything, to stand firm.*

—32—

ALREADY BLESSED

Most of us ask God for His blessings nearly every time we pray. But did you know that in grace, God has already supplied everything you need? Grace is all that God has done for you, and He can do nothing new for you or more for you than He's already done. Ephesians 1:3 says, "Blessed be the God and Father of our Lord Jesus Christ, who has blessed us with every spiritual blessing in the heavenly places in Christ."

But if God has already blessed each of us through His grace, where are our blessings? The verse we just read tells us they are located in the heavenly places. Part of living victoriously in spiritual warfare, as you are seeing in our time together in this devotional, involves realigning your vision so you look at heavenly places more often. Once you see that your blessings are already there, you realize that accessing them isn't necessarily about asking. It's more about believing in faith that they are yours. God has already provided. Your faith is what grabs your blessings and brings them down—including your blessings of victory in spiritual battles.

Faith might involve asking in prayer. But it also may simply involve believing that what God has given to you is already yours. Each situation will be different. Just remember that belief is critical to claiming your victory as you walk through each day—belief that God has given you every spiritual blessing in the heavenly places.

2 CORINTHIANS 5:7 *For we walk by faith, not by sight.*

—33—

WHOSE TRUTH IS TRUE?

Jesus said that the truth will set you free. Do you know what it is like to live free, or are you constantly in a struggle? Living free means you experience each day with the full goodness and grace of God flowing through you. You are not bound by worry, doubt, shame, or regret, some of the things Satan uses to keep believers from living in spiritual freedom.

The problem today is that there are so many variations on what people consider to be true. An accountant, a psychologist, and a lawyer were together one day discussing truth. The psychologist said truth is what you feel it to be. The accountant said truth is what you need it to be. And of course, the lawyer said truth is what you want it to be.

Our world is full of opinions, prognostications, and perceptions. Coffee is bad for you, they say. That is, until another study comes out saying coffee is good for you. You can apply this to so many things we consume and, over time, it's difficult to know what is truly true.

Only God can be the fixed standard of what is true because He is the creator of everything. God is the definer of truth. When you live by what He says, you will know what true freedom is like.

JOHN 18:38 *Pilate said to Him, "What is truth?" And when he had said this, he went out again to the Jews and said to them, "I find no guilt in Him."*

—34—

GO FISH

Knowing truth and living according to truth will help you along your way to victory in spiritual battles. Yet while truth includes facts, you can still have facts without truth. Truth is much more than facts.

It's like the man who went fishing and brought home twenty catfish. He said to his wife, "I caught twenty catfish today!" She asked him how he caught the fish.

He replied, "Well, I went to the fish market and told the guy to throw me twenty catfish! Then, I caught them!" Now, it's true that the man gave the facts. The problem is that he didn't tell the truth. Rather, he configured the facts so he could hide the truth.

Truth includes much more than facts. It also includes the intent of the facts. That's why the Bible says when you come before God, you are to lift your veil in full disclosure. You are not to come with a hidden face or seeking to manipulate God in what you say. God knows the truth. And just as He wants you to come to Him in truth, He also wants you to live according to the truth He has supplied. When you do both, you are well on your way to spiritual victory in your life.

2 CORINTHIANS 3:18 *But we all, with unveiled face, beholding as in a mirror the glory of the Lord, are being transformed into the same image from glory to glory, just as from the Lord, the Spirit.*

—35—

HITTING BACK WITH TRUTH

The demonic spiritual realm can't handle the truth, which wages war against its lies and deception. That's why it's important to know the truth. You can't successfully battle against the enemy if you don't use the right weapons, and one of the primary weapons is the truth of God.

When Jesus was being attacked by the devil, we read in Matthew 4 that He hit him three times with the truth, responding with, "It is written." Each time, Jesus followed up with what had been written in Scripture. The devil left Him after that because Satan couldn't handle the truth.

Satan thrives in a world of chaos and confusion. His nature is steeped in lies. That's why when you are under spiritual attack, you are often confused or thinking things that are farfetched. Over time, though, those things don't seem so farfetched because Satan can get you thinking something for so long that it begins to feel true to you. However, when you tell someone else about it, they will often be able to see right through it. That's why accountability is so critical. Being open about your struggles and what you believe to be true is important to living in victory.

Spiritual accountability allows others to speak truth into your life and into any confusion you are facing. Once you come back to the truth, you can hit the devil with it just like Jesus did. Then the devil will flee.

JOHN 8:32 *And you will know the truth, and the truth will make you free.*

—36—

THE BONDAGE OF GUILT

One of the ways Satan keeps a person in bondage is through guilt. To understand guilt, we need to first understand righteousness. Righteousness is simply the standard that God requires for people to become acceptable to Him. That standard is predicated on the truth, which is whatever God says about a matter. The truth is the truth, regardless of how many people disagree about it.

Righteousness is our response to God's standard. In basketball, the goal is ten feet high. If you lower the goal, you've lowered the standard. Many attempt to lower God's standard, shoot the shot, and think they accomplished something impressive if they make the goal. But they simply have adjusted the standard to a level they could meet.

But God doesn't negotiate His standard. His standard is His standard. We can't lower it. And when we fail to reach it, we have sinned. All of us have sinned, which Romans 3:23 plainly states. This is why Christ's atonement is absolutely critical. But not only did Christ cover our sins, He also removed our guilt. Spiritual struggles arise when we continue to operate under a covering of shame and guilt. It is easy to do so, especially since we live in a largely judgmental culture. But that's exactly what Satan wants—to keep each of us bound by a guilt that God himself released us from through the sacrifice on the cross.

ROMANS 8:1 *Therefore there is now no condemnation for those who are in Christ Jesus.*

—37—

HIDING THE TRASH

There's a big difference between *looking* clean and *being* clean—not just in housekeeping, but in life as well. If you have someone coming over to your house, you usually want it to appear clean. So sometimes, you'll toss things in a closet or spare room. Then you shut the door. Your house isn't clean. It just looks clean.

Many believers do the same with sin: They stuff their sins away and put on their best face for others, thinking they have fooled everyone. They hide their junk and clutter, hoping everyone thinks they don't have any. We would be naïve to think that about anyone, really. But even if people don't know about your hidden trash, God does. He will continue to weigh on your conscience until you come clean before Him. That doesn't mean you have to tell everyone else the details of your garbage (even if they ask). But it does mean you need to repent before God and seek His healing in your life. Big or small, trash stinks. So does sin. Allowing it to go unaddressed is one way Satan entangles you in even more sin. Keeping your spiritual life clean before the Lord allows Him to work and battle on your behalf, and on behalf of the advancement of His glory.

ROMANS 2:4 *Or do you think lightly of the riches of His kindness and tolerance and patience, not knowing that the kindness of God leads you to repentance?*

—38—

PAIN CAN BE POSITIVE

I went on a cruise a number of years ago and had a terrible toothache. In fact, the tooth hurt so much that I couldn't eat. Not eating on a cruise is painful in and of itself! Even though I was taking over-the-counter medicine for the toothache, it just wouldn't go away. That's when I opted for calling my dentist in Dallas. After listening to me go on and on about my symptoms, he told me I had an infection.

All the over-the-counter medicine did was mask for a time the pain caused by the infection. But then the pain would always come back because it was there to tell me something. If I had ignored such a serious infection, it could have turned deadly. But because the pain was so present, I couldn't ignore it.

None of us like to feel pain. But pain can be used by God to reveal areas within us that are infected. Maybe it's sin or temptation you need to address. It could be something within your relationships that needs adjusting. God knows what you need and when you need it. He also knows how easy it is to ignore Him when life is going well. Always pay attention to spiritual pain. It can be used by God to strengthen you and sharpen you so that you can be more capable of living victoriously against the devil's schemes.

ROMANS 5:3 *And not only this, but we also exult in our tribulations, knowing that tribulation brings about perseverance.*

— 39 —

SEARCH WITHIN

Religion is usually about changing what we do on the outside in hopes that it will change us on the inside. But true spiritual growth in Christianity works the other way around. Let's say I gave you one hundred thousand dollars by transferring it into your bank account. As soon as I tell you that, if you believe me, you are going to open your bank account app or stop by your bank to verify it. You will do this because something of value has been given to you.

Similarly, when you were saved, God deposited within your soul all the righteousness that belongs to Jesus Christ. But you can't benefit from it unless you know it's there. Oftentimes, we look for external ways to become righteous or to check off a list that says we are good enough. But God tells us that true righteousness is within us, accessed through a real, authentic relationship with Him (Luke 17:21).

There's nothing that keeps a person more ineffective in spiritual battles than a presumed righteousness based on external measures. There's no power in that. Your strength for spiritual warfare comes from the relationship you have with God, and the connection to Christ within you through the Holy Spirit.

MATTHEW 6:33 *But seek first His kingdom and His righteousness, and all these things will be added to you.*

—40—

SENSELESS PEACE

It's perfectly logical to be at peace when everything around you is calm and tranquil. But the kind of peace Jesus promises often makes no sense—a senseless peace that you get in the midst of spiritual battles, or the peace that stretches beyond your comprehension. God provides peace to those whose hearts are committed to Him, but you need to know what God's peace is like to make the most of it.

Two painters were asked to paint a picture for a contest. The subject was peace. The first painter created a serene scene: The sun was glistening off the lake so you could see the shine across the water. The water was still, almost like glass. The painting even included a shepherd walking sheep nearby.

In the second painter's picture, the sky was pitch-black. The waves on the water billowed, and boats were being tossed about. It was a portrait of disaster! Yet in the corner, just on the edge of this horrific circumstance, a little bird perched on a rock. Its mouth was open, and a tiny light came up into the darkness—the bird's song.

You might be surprised to learn that the painter who won the contest was the second painter. Peace doesn't mean you won't have problems. Peace means your problems won't have you. That's biblical peace. Peace is not the absence of spiritual warfare, but rather the strength and calm to stabilize you within it.

ISAIAH 26:3 *The steadfast of mind You will keep in perfect peace, because he trusts in You.*

If you are not ruled by peace, you are a victim of the spiritual battles around you.

—41—

PUNCTUATED BY PEACE

Your life ought to be punctuated by a spirit of peace if you are walking with the Spirit. Colossians 3:15 says, "Let the peace of Christ rule in your hearts, to which indeed you were called in one body; and be thankful." The Greek word translated "rule" here means to umpire. An umpire calls a game according to how that game aligns with the rules. Whether a pitcher throws a strike or a ball is called by the umpire—and whatever the umpire calls is final.

We are to let the peace of Christ have the final say in our lives. If you are not ruled by peace, you are a victim of the spiritual battles around you. You have fallen prey to Satan's attack. Measuring your level of peace is a great way to gauge how successful you are in spiritual warfare. Christ's calm within you can remain steady when you are waging spiritual warfare according to God's Word.

Part of the armor of God we are to wear are the shoes of peace (Ephesians 6:15). No matter where you walk or how treacherous the road, if you walk in shoes of peace, you will remain steady and will not fall. You will not lose your bearings or get lost. A life punctuated by peace, despite all that is conspiring and transpiring around you to cause anxiety, is a life ruled by Jesus Christ.

2 THESSALONIANS 3:16 *Now may the Lord of peace Himself continually grant you peace in every circumstance. The Lord be with you all!*

—42—

GOING DEEP

No matter how tough things get on the outside, God guarantees peace on the inside when we seek Him and His righteousness. Putting God first and trusting in Him gives you access to the peace you desire.

Submarines don't have to get nervous in a storm. The deeper they go, the less impact the storm has on them. Similarly, fish don't have to suffer from nervous attacks during storms. They know that no matter how bad the storm is on the surface, all they have to do is swim deep enough to avoid it. It's calm down in the depths of the sea. Even the worst storm can't reach them there.

Submarines and fish go deep when things get chaotic up top. When your world gets chaotic, it's a reminder to you that it's time to go deep too. It's time to dip down into God's presence in ways you never have before. You will find calm in His presence. You will find peace in His presence. You will find courage to overcome. Because down there in the depth of God's presence, the perfect mind of God is made manifest in your spirit. When you retreat into Him, you will be refreshed. Isaiah 26:3 says, "The steadfast of mind You will keep in perfect peace, because he trusts in You."

PHILIPPIANS 4:7 *And the peace of God, which surpasses all comprehension, will guard your hearts and your minds in Christ Jesus.*

—43—

PEACE IN THE FURNACE

God has the power to help you keep your cool when things around you heat up. Look at the story of Shadrach, Meshach, and Abed-nego. Because they refused to bow before the idol King Nebuchadnezzar had set up, the king decided to have them thrown into the fiery furnace. Most people would be filled with anxiety, fear, and dread. Yet these men remained steadfast.

Daniel 3:17–18 says, "Shadrach, Meshach and Abed-nego replied to the king, ". . . our God whom we serve is able to deliver us from the furnace of blazing fire; and He will deliver us out of your hand, O king. But even if He does not, let it be known to you, O king, that we are not going to serve your gods or worship the golden image that you have set up."

The men knew that God could deliver them. But they also knew that if God chose not to deliver them, He was still good. He had a reason and a purpose for their pain. Their faith enabled them to face and survive the fiery trial. God sent Jesus to join them in the fire, and ultimately released them unscathed. Living in faith rather than in fear enables you to escape the fiery darts Satan throws your way. Lift up your shield of faith as you follow God.

DANIEL 3:25 *He said, "Look! I see four men loosed and walking about in the midst of the fire without harm, and the appearance of the fourth is like a son of the gods!"*

—44—

LYING EMOTIONS

Have you ever been tricked by your emotions? It's like when you are watching a scary movie, and even though you know the antagonists in the movie aren't real, you still get chills when you see them. You still shriek when they jump out of hiding. You still look away if they come at the screen.

It doesn't matter that you know in your mind that nothing on the screen is real or true; your emotions respond as if it is. This is because emotions do not need truth. In fact, emotions are easily manipulated. What's more, the media masters know this. They write or create movies, songs, and entertainment in a way that will keep you coming back for more. What's worse, Satan knows this too.

If you want to be astute in spiritual warfare and wise against the enemy's attacks, you are going to have to learn to question your emotions. You need to put them in a grid of God's truth to see if they are accurate or not. At times they will be accurate. But other times, they will not. God's Word will let you know.

As long as you allow your emotions to control or dominate you, you will lack the fundamental building blocks of faith. Faith is necessary for overcoming the enemy's schemes in your life.

2 CORINTHIANS 10:7 *You are looking at things as they are outwardly. If anyone is confident in himself that he is Christ's, let him consider this again within himself, that just as he is Christ's, so also are we.*

—45—

FAITH IS AN ACTION

Faith involves more than just what you believe, more than agreeing with the truth, more than what you say. Faith involves your feet. For example, if you went to the doctor because you had a stomachache, the doctor would not just take your word for it. He or she would order some tests to help them determine what was wrong. Then, when the tests revealed the cause, they would give you medication.

Now, if you accepted the truth that the medication would help you but you did not take the medication, would the medication help you? Or if you received the written prescription for the medication you needed but you did nothing with the prescription and it remained in your car, would that prescription help you? You get the point. Believing the truth and knowing the truth are just part of faith. Faith always involves action. Without obedience to the revealed truth, you will continue to suffer stomach pain.

The shield of faith is one part of the armor of God. It is a critical piece in carrying out victorious spiritual warfare. But it must be accompanied by the other pieces to move you forward in battle. You must walk by faith in your shoes of peace. You must take steps in obedience to what God has told you. Fighting the good fight is more than just a one-step move. Like any good fight, you need a multiplicity of maneuvers to outwit and outbattle the opponent.

HEBREWS 11:1 *Now faith is the assurance of things hoped for, the conviction of things not seen.*

—46—

SIN MANAGEMENT

You and I are engaged in a spiritual battle. Awareness of this truth is half the battle. But once you become aware, you need to start fighting well. And until you address the invisible spiritual cause of any matter you face in the physical realm, you can never fully address its visible and physical manifestation.

The unfortunate problem today is that most of us address our physical and visible problems in physical and visible ways. But if you spend all your time addressing the physical and visible manifestations of flesh and blood, and very little of your time dealing with the invisible spiritual cause, the best thing you can do is to manage the problem. You will not fix it.

So much of our defeat, frustration, misery, anguish, agony, and difficulty comes from the fact that we are forgetting where our spiritual battles take place. We have forgotten the fact that the spiritual realm, and primarily our ability to function in it, determines how well we succeed in this physical world. Scripture says that we died with Jesus Christ, we were buried with Him, we were raised with Him, and now we are seated with Him in heavenly places. (See Ephesians 2:6.) We are now living spiritually with Jesus in another realm. Until and unless you operate in and from this spiritual realm, you will remain controlled by the physical realm.

EPHESIANS 2:7 *So that in the ages to come He might show the surpassing riches of His grace in kindness toward us in Christ Jesus.*

—47—

FAITH, TRUTH, AND ACTION

I often define faith as acting like something is so even when it is not so in order that it might be so simply because God said so. The key word in that statement is *acting*. To take action. Essentially, faith is acting on the assumption that God is telling you the truth. If you don't know the truth, you can't act on it. Discovering the truth of God's Word should be a priority for you. And once you do know the truth, you must act on it. Apply it. Let it be the dominant factor in your choices.

The truth is always God's view on a matter. If you are not interested in identifying God's perspective, then you are not interested in gaining victory in spiritual battles. Just as a boxing coach gives advice during a match, God gives you the truth on what to do. He, as your coach, is there to guide you in how to fight the good fight.

Because your feelings are often circumstantially driven, you cannot rely on them. You should not act on them. You must dig deep and unearth the truth rooted in God. That's how you win each spiritual battle.

MATTHEW 21:21 *And Jesus answered and said to them, "Truly I say to you, if you have faith and do not doubt, you will not only do what was done to the fig tree, but even if you say to this mountain, 'Be taken up and cast into the sea,' it will happen."*

—48—

RECOGNIZING WHAT'S REAL

Our brains pick up clues to help us distinguish what is real and what isn't. But there is one critical piece of evidence we often overlook or ignore. We sometimes call it a sixth sense. It's your spirit's ability to discern wisdom and truth. When your spirit is closely connected to the Holy Spirit, you will tap into this wisdom. But if you allow your brain to solely rely on your five senses, you will wind up confused.

Faith can't be based on empirical evidence alone or it's no longer faith. Hebrews 11:1 defines faith for us: "Now faith is the assurance of things hoped for, the conviction of things not seen." So faith can't be based on what you have seen. God desires to reward your faith, but it must be true faith.

The point of faith is to grab something from the unseen realm and bring it into the visible realm. You never start with what you see. Oftentimes, faith asks you to start with the opposite of what you see. While things might appear one way, God may be asking you to believe and trust Him that they are an entirely other way. He's asking you to believe Him, but that belief is demonstrated through actions. Rely on your belief in God and His Word as you begin to increase your faith walk with the Lord.

HEBREWS 11:3 *By faith we understand that the worlds were prepared by the word of God, so that what is seen was not made out of things which are visible.*

49

TAKE OUT THE TRASH

It's good to take out the trash. If you leave it to sit, it becomes an invitation for roaches to hang out. It invites more dirt and filth into your home. Not only does the trash start to smell over time, but it also attracts more destructive things like ants and mold. In short, your trash issue turns into a varmint issue before long. And even if you don't add any more garbage to the heap, the ants, roaches, and varmints will continue to multiply.

Sin can do the same thing. The reason people address sin in their life from years ago is because the spiritual devastation that sin caused has continued, even if the sin has stopped. The consequences of sin—even sin you have ceased—show up as demonic influence and attack. The way to address sin, even sin committed years ago, is to ask God to clean up your spiritual life and get rid of the trash that has welcomed greater demonic influence or increased spiritual battles.

Repenting isn't only for things you might be doing right now, but can also be for things you did a long time ago. Ask God to reveal to you any areas of your past you need to repent of so He can take out the trash you've allowed to accumulate.

GENESIS 6:13 *Then God said to Noah, "The end of all flesh has come before Me; for the earth is filled with violence because of them; and behold, I am about to destroy them with the earth."*

—50—

OFFENSIVE COORDINATOR

Sometimes when we are on the front lines of spiritual warfare, it can feel like we are out there all alone. But that's far from the truth. Let me explain through this illustration. In a football game, the quarterback is the leader on the field. The quarterback is calling the plays and setting the agenda. The quarterback is always under attack. The opposing defense is always trying to get him—sack him, knock him down, block him, move him out of the pocket, and anything else they can do to make him ineffective.

The quarterback might feel alone but he is not. High above in a booth or on the sidelines is his offensive coordinator, whose job is to tell the quarterback what he should be doing, especially in light of what's coming at him. With today's technology, plays can be spoken right into the quarterback's helmet.

Paul says that for this spiritual battle we are waging, we are to put on the helmet of salvation (Ephesians 6:17). This helmet gives us direct access to Jesus Christ. Yes, the enemy is attacking us. But God wants us to put on a helmet so He can speak the wisdom, moves, and plays into our minds. He sits on high and can see the whole field. He can see much better than you or I ever could. Listen to Him. You might feel alone, but you are not alone in this battle.

PROVERBS 3:6 *In all your ways acknowledge Him, and He will make your paths straight.*

— 51 —

NULLIFYING FAITH

All of us have sinned. Each of us has made poor choices and wound up regretting it. Only Jesus never sinned. So it is important to be honest when we have sinned, to allow ourselves to be held accountable and accept the consequences so we can learn from them and move on. Because when we let sin creep into our lives and remain there, we don't realize what comes creeping in along with it.

You might think that by hiding your sin you won't face consequences. But there are spiritual consequences—and those often are worse than the ones you suffer when coming clean. Sure, your reputation may take a hit when you repent, but your spiritual life will be healed. And your spiritual life is what matters most for eternity.

Remember, you and I are saved by grace through faith. Why would we need a Savior if we never sinned? To think that someone never sins is ridiculous. Too often we put other people, and even ourselves, on a pedestal. Jesus died for all of us. That's what salvation means. We are to seek righteousness and pursue God and His kingdom agenda in all we do, but we are also not to deceive ourselves into thinking that Jesus plus our righteousness gets us to heaven, or gets us victory in battle. Jesus' grace is given freely from the cross. We are all equal at the foot of His cross.

EPHESIANS 2:8 *For by grace you have been saved through faith; and that not of yourselves, it is the gift of God.*

—52—

RELATIONSHIP TRANSACTIONS

Usually, the more you do for somebody, the more they grow to like you. But your relationship with God doesn't work that way at all. What's different? Salvation means we are to relate to God based on grace—based on what Jesus did, not on our own performance.

You do not have to try to get God to like you. That's wasted energy. You do not have to think, *If I do this—or don't do this—God will love me more*. All the love God is ever going to have for you, He already has. Once you realize that, you can live more spiritually free.

Now, I realize that most of us were raised in homes or in a culture that reinforced the need to earn people's favor, and far too many of us have become people pleasers as a result. But that mindset is damaging when we carry it into our relationship with God. What Jesus Christ did on the cross is the full demonstration of God's grace and His love. Could you do anything more than that?

Humility is at the heart of tapping into God's grace. When you humbly realize you are a sinner saved by grace—and that there are no special saints in God's kingdom—you will see God show up for you in ways you never imagined. And you will gain the strength you need to fight the good fight of faith.

PSALM 5:12 *For it is You who blesses the righteous man, O LORD, You surround him with favor as with a shield.*

— 53 —

WITNESS PROTECTION

When we come to God by faith, He changes us. And that change often goes a lot deeper than we think. The United States has what is known as a witness protection program, which changes the identity of witnesses so they can be safe if someone is after them.

This program provides a new name, social security number, driver's license, job, and a place to live—even new identities for family members, if needed. The witness is reclassified in the best way possible to keep their enemy from harming them.

God also has a witness protection program of sorts. See, Satan is after you. You are a testimony to the grace of Jesus Christ. When you testify of your salvation to the world, you bring attention to yourself. The demons take notice. They desire to harm you. But God has changed your identity so that you are now identified with Jesus Christ. Galatians 2:20 says, "I have been crucified with Christ; and it is no longer I who live, but Christ lives in me; and the life which I now live in the flesh I live by faith in the Son of God, who loved me and gave Himself up for me."

When your identity is that of Jesus Christ, you gain access to the power and kingdom authority He has. But to fully do so, you need to let go of your old ways and embrace your new identity in Jesus.

GALATIANS 2:19 *For through the Law I died to the Law, so that I might live to God.*

— 54 —

VIRTUAL REALITY

A lot of the so-called "realities" we've come to accept in today's culture turn out to be illusions when you start digging, or lift the curtain. You know what virtual reality is? This technology allows you to put on goggles that make it seem like you are in a different place. These days, you can get all this fancy stuff that makes you think you are somewhere you are not. In fact, it can even initiate feelings to correspond with what you are seeing through the goggles.

What you see through the goggles might look and feel real, but it's not. It's not authentic. Yet because it feels real, you might scream or laugh or lean as though it is real. You act like it's real. The enemy wants to put you in a virtual reality so you operate in what you think is real and what you feel is real, even though it's not real. The enemy wants to dupe you, manipulate you, and deceive you. That's his main goal. Paul said that if you are going to win against enemy attacks, you must stand firm. Not only that, but you must also have on your helmet of salvation. You must wear your helmet of salvation and not virtual reality goggles given to you by the evil one. Your mind must be covered with the saving knowledge of God's Word.

1 TIMOTHY 6:12 *Fight the good fight of faith; take hold of the eternal life to which you were called, and you made the good confession in the presence of many witnesses.*

—55—

THE HELMET OF SALVATION

The armor of God mentioned in the book of Ephesians describes ways God has equipped us to fight the good fight in the spiritual battles we face. But there is one piece of armor we often underuse. It's the helmet of salvation.

So what exactly is this helmet you are supposed to put over your head, mind, and your thinking? How do you put on "salvation"? At the core of most of our problems is our lack of understanding of the word *salvation*. *Salvation* is a word that summarizes all that Christ has provided for us. And just so you know, batteries are included.

Paul said in Romans 1:16, "For I am not ashamed of the gospel, for it is the power of God for salvation to everyone who believes, to the Jew first and also to the Greek." Salvation is the delivering power of God. Not only does salvation deliver you from hell in the future, but salvation also delivers you from hell in the present. It's not a literal hell, but oftentimes life can feel like you are going through hell. If that describes you, you don't have your helmet on. When addictions, emotions, people, worries, concerns, and all else rule over you, then you don't have your helmet on. Salvation is the deliverance power we all need to live freely in spiritual victory each day.

ROMANS 1:17 *For in it the righteousness of God is revealed from faith to faith; as it is written, "But the righteous man shall live by faith."*

—56—

PRAYER DEFINED

Ask most people to define prayer and they will tell you it is talking to God. But there is so much more to it than that. One of the toughest things God has to do is to get His people to look at life, and live life, from a spiritual frame of reference. Prayer involves much more than just talking to God because it is essentially a realignment of your mental state from earthly to eternal. It allows your mind to move from the physical presence reality to the spiritual presence of God.

Ephesians 6:18 follows up the description of the armor of God by telling us what we are to do once we have put it on: "With all prayer and petition pray at all times in the Spirit, and with this in view, be on the alert with all perseverance and petition for all the saints." You are to pray at all times. That doesn't mean shutting yourself in a room and praying twenty-four hours a day. It means that you are to orient your thinking toward God's perspective, being in communion with Him at all times. Then you will begin to view life through His lens.

Prayer calls on God to intervene in ways He wants to intervene anyway, but wouldn't do until requested. One way to know how God wants to intervene is through continually abiding with Him.

EPHESIANS 6:19 *And pray on my behalf, that utterance may be given to me in the opening of my mouth, to make known with boldness the mystery of the gospel.*

— 57 —

WHAT PRAYER DOES

Some people think of God as a heavenly vending machine. You drop in a prayer or two, and out pops whatever you want. But prayer is not making God do something He never planned to do. Rather, prayer is grabbing something God intended to do and dragging it down to earth.

It's important to realize that what God intends to do doesn't always happen on earth just because it's intended in heaven. The Christian walk and the spiritual battles we face are participatory in nature. We have been given free will, and with that gift comes responsibility.

God's preferred will happens on earth when it is grabbed by those on earth through the participation of faith and prayer. Your problems and battles exist in heavenly places along with your blessings. Prayer takes you there. Unfortunately, far too many of us spend all our time talking to men about God, and very little time talking to God about men. We spend a lot of time talking to others about our circumstances, maybe even looking for sympathy. But what you need are answers, not sympathy. What you need is for heaven to invade earth through this thing called prayer. Prayer is not making God do something. But prayer enables you to receive what God intends to give. One thing we know He intends to give you is victory over the evil one. The victory is already yours. You can pull it down through prayer.

COLOSSIANS 4:2 *Devote yourselves to prayer, keeping alert in it with an attitude of thanksgiving.*

—58—

GETTING THE SIGNAL

Music plays over the radio and television and on streaming services. But you can't hear the music unless you tune in to the station or tap into Wi-Fi. Without accessing the technology that can pull the sounds from the airwaves and that can supply it to you, the music remains unheard. In short, you need something in the physical realm to access the invisible.

But even if you don't tap into the airwaves, they still exist and operate invisibly around you. If you do not have music playing right now, or if you are only tuned in to one station, that doesn't eliminate the myriad options available in the invisible realm. Similarly, just because you do not tap into what you need in the spiritual realm does not mean it isn't there. God is right here with us. His Holy Spirit is moving in the spiritual realm all around us. God's angels are also moving, and willing to help you wage victorious warfare.

You can't access the music available in air just by wanting to. You need a device designed to do so. This is similar to the spiritual realm. Even though angels and demons exist all around us, accessing the angelic help you need comes through intentional prayer to God. Prayer enables you to contact the invisible spiritual realm, bringing its reality into the visible, physical realm in which you battle.

PSALM 145:18 *The Lord is near to all who call upon Him, to all who call upon Him in truth.*

— 59 —

EYES OPEN

Some of us have been taught that prayer starts with a three-part process: bowing your head, folding your hands, and closing your eyes. But the Bible paints a different picture of the posture of prayer. In fact, most prayers depicted in the Bible were not carried out with eyes closed. Most of the time, the Bible says, they lifted their eyes. Not only were their eyes open, but they were lifted up.

First Peter 5:8 gives us insight too: "Be of sober spirit, be on the alert. Your adversary, the devil, prowls around like a roaring lion, seeking someone to devour." It's hard to be on the alert with your eyes closed. We are to keep our eyes open to Satan's schemes and view prayer as more than a moment to meditate. To pray continually involves praying throughout your day, important because your enemy is a roaring lion. As you may know, lions roar when they have conquered a territory or rival. In other words, it's their declaration of victory.

When you talk to God, you are giving heaven permission to battle Satan on your behalf. You are engaging in spiritual warfare. You are actively seeking assistance. Pray more throughout your day. Yes, it's good to pray with your eyes closed at times. But also consider praying throughout your day with your eyes open. Call on the Lord in times of need, and He will respond.

JEREMIAH 33:3 *Call to Me and I will answer you, and I will tell you great and mighty things, which you do not know.*

—60—

PRAYING SPECIFICALLY

Sometimes it seems as though God stops hearing our prayers just when we need Him most. But the problem may be much closer to home. One of the reasons we don't see God show up in the midst of our struggles is that we don't talk honestly to God when we need Him. Perhaps we forget. Or maybe we don't take prayer seriously.

Too many of us offer vague prayers. We toss up prayers we have committed to memory. Some people approach prayer like a checklist, not like a weapon in spiritual warfare. But when all hell breaks loose, you learn how to pray differently. When all hell breaks loose in your life, you obtain a unique ability to get very specific in your prayers. Prayer is no longer a routine.

To pray in the spirit means you are making a spiritual connection to God. You can do that by quoting Scripture in your prayer, or taking a principle from His Word and praying it. You can do it by worshiping God or calling on His attributes to be made known in your life. Praying in the spirit—connecting with God's Holy Spirit—involves pushing past the routine prayers you've memorized to a true conversation with God. Doing this enables you to hear from God and engage in spiritual warfare at a deeper, more effective level.

PHILIPPIANS 4:6 *Be anxious for nothing, but in everything by prayer and supplication with thanksgiving let your requests be made known to God.*

—61—

THE FLESH CAN'T FIX THE FLESH

The reason human-based solutions can't always break physical addictions lies in the root of these physical addictions.

Whether it is alcoholism, drugs, pornography, or gluttony, far too many men find themselves caught in and unable to break free from sin's grasp. In fact, there is a whole addiction industry today that employs professionals to help people get out of the vise grip illegitimately holding them hostage. Yet most of the solutions offered in this industry rely on the flesh to free the flesh. And while that may work for a time, what typically happens is that one addiction is replaced by another. Have you ever overcome something only to discover you simply shifted your focus or obsession to a new stronghold? That is very common when we aim to fix the flesh with the flesh.

As a reminder, a stronghold is a spiritually based addiction. It means that if you try to fix an addiction—which is really a stronghold—without the right spiritual connection, success won't last. You can't be released from it because you haven't dealt with the core issue behind it. You need to strengthen your spiritual life by addressing the core spiritual root of life's issues.

REVELATION 1:5 *And from Jesus Christ, the faithful witness, the first-born of the dead, and the ruler of the kings of the earth. To Him who loves us and released us from our sins by His blood.*

—62—

DECORATED PRISONS

When a person becomes caught in the grip of a stronghold, true freedom seems elusive. One way Satan seeks to defeat believers is by leading them into a pit of hopelessness. If the pit becomes so deep that a true recovery can no longer be seen, people often give up. Remember, Satan does not have spiritual authority over you. But he can bully you, threaten you, and deceive you into thinking he does. When you give up the battle, you have given in to Satan's lies.

Those who struggle with addictions and strongholds might understand when I say that it can feel like you are in prison and someone has thrown away the key. What many people do in their hopelessness is accept the situation as inevitable. Since they see no way out of their prison cell, they make the mistake of decorating it, of calling it home. They settle for their cell.

But God wants you to live free from oppression and sin's restraint. Whether it is a sin you are presently committing that you need freedom from or the consequences of a sin you committed years ago, the starting point to living in freedom is confession. Let God know that you know you fell short. Then allow yourself to go through the redemptive and healing process that must take place, no matter how humbling that may be. Never let pride keep you in the prison of sin or a past sin's consequences.

PSALM 31:24 *Be strong and let your heart take courage, all you who hope in the Lord.*

—63—

WHOM SHOULD YOU LISTEN TO?

You wouldn't ask your auto mechanic to do brain surgery on you. I'm sure he's good with his hands, but brain surgery requires a different set of skills. Yet, how many people seek help every day from those who don't know what they're talking about? Just because someone claims to be an expert or has a large following on a streaming platform or social media doesn't make them an expert. When it comes to wisdom for your life, you need to consult the ultimate authority living right inside of you.

Jesus calls himself the "Alpha and the Omega" for a reason. He is to be the sum total of your knowledge base. Even in biblical times, those who had people skills or charisma knew how to manipulate a following. That's why Paul reminded the church at Colossae that Jesus is to be the totality of our wisdom. It says in Colossians 2:2–4, "Attaining to all the wealth that comes from the full assurance of understanding, resulting in a true knowledge of God's mystery, that is, Christ Himself, in whom are hidden all the treasures of wisdom and knowledge. I say this so that no one will delude you with persuasive argument."

Be cautious who you gain life advice from, especially since the greatest wisdom for waging victorious spiritual warfare is near to you in the person of Jesus Christ.

REVELATION 1:8 *I am the Alpha and the Omega, says the Lord God, who is and who was and who is to come, the Almighty.*

—64—

FIGHTING THE FLESH

While salvation happens in an instant, the process known as *sanctification*, learning to live a holy life, takes time. You don't have to be saved for long to know that when you got saved, your flesh didn't disappear. For those of us whose flesh was well-trained before being saved, our salvation was a new opportunity for our flesh to show how strong it really is.

Even the apostle Paul struggled with something he couldn't shake. In Romans 7:14–24, he writes of doing things he did not want to do. He told himself he shouldn't do it. He let us know in his writing that the desire not to do it was there. He was serious about wanting to stop whatever it was, but he didn't have the ability to pull it off.

When someone like Paul can admit to struggling and losing battles with his flesh from time to time, shouldn't that give all of us the insight that no one other than Jesus is purely righteous? Shouldn't that encourage us to show one another the same grace we desire or need for ourselves? Paul struggled between his flesh and his spirit. The two simply did not get along. Paul's acknowledgement ought to help the body of Christ be less quick to judge someone else. It's difficult to throw stones when your hands, and heart, are serving the Lord.

ROMANS 7:15 *For what I am doing, I do not understand; for I am not practicing what I would like to do, but I am doing the very thing I hate.*

— 65 —

DUELING DIETS

Even if you have an appetite for spiritual things, *other* appetites can cancel it out. Even when you desire to live a righteous life, other desires in your flesh can override that, as Paul stated in Romans 7. Living a spiritual life is a daily battle. You can't let down your guard. It's not something that comes naturally to any of us.

Have you ever gone to a restaurant for some delicious but unhealthy food, only to order a diet drink to go with it? Somehow, the thought is that a diet drink will cancel out the fat and sugar in the meal. But a diet drink does nothing to reduce the impact of fried chicken, mac and cheese, sweet potato pie, and potato salad. We know that to be true. But what too many people think is that attending church on Sunday will cancel out the negative consequences that come through indulging the flesh on a regular basis.

Whether it is simply watching a show you shouldn't, listening to music that is unrighteous, or talking to the person who always emphasizes the world and its worldview as the right one, indulging your flesh enough times in those ways will ultimately catch up to you. No amount of Sunday church attendance will cancel it out. You have to learn how to make the tough choices rooted in self-restraint about what thoughts and conversations you allow to enter your mind.

GALATIANS 5:23 *Gentleness, self-control; against such things there is no law.*

—66—

WHICH TRUTH SETS US FREE?

Some people think the definition of truth has changed. And while that might be true for our culture, it isn't true overall. The definition of truth remains the same as it always has been. God is the Creator of the universe in which we live, and as the Creator, He determines the truth. He sets the rules. He establishes how things run. If you want to make up the rules or live by your own truth, then you need to go make your own universe. God has made this one, so He is in charge.

In John 8:31–32, we read a very powerful passage: "So Jesus was saying to those Jews who had believed Him, 'If you continue in My word, then you are truly disciples of Mine; and you will know the truth, and the truth will make you free.'" It's important to note that the passage says *the* truth, not your truth or my truth. The only truth that will work as a weapon in spiritual battle is *the* truth. Satan and his demons will laugh at your truth or my truth. It's only God's truth that defeats him. Keep that in mind as you wage spiritual warfare so you don't rely on something that has no power to defend you. Only the truth carries the kingdom authority that can defeat the realm of darkness in your life.

PSALM 24:1 *The earth is the Lord's, and all it contains, the world, and those who dwell in it.*

—67—

WASHBOARDS

Have you ever gotten a stain in your clothes that you couldn't get out? Some stains won't come out using regular detergent and require a bit of elbow grease. They require a good old-fashioned washboard to scrub it on. Some effects from sin are the same way. It requires commitment to remove not only the stronghold but also the resultant consequences in your life, or the lives of those impacted.

Sin remains Satan's first strategy for entanglement in spiritual warfare. If he can trap you in sin, he has you on a lot of levels. The effects of sin—the strains in your relationships, work, finances—can greatly compound the harm and reach of the original sin. That's why it is so important to maintain personal righteousness. You must engage in a daily spiritual battle to live a righteous life. You can't set your life on autopilot or hit the cruise-control button. You must show up every day because Satan will seek to trip you up when you least expect it.

To live victoriously over sin and free yourself from its stains and negative results, you must surrender to the lordship of Jesus Christ. You must make His Word and His truth the ruling force over all you do, think, and say. When you live this way, you will win the battle every day.

ROMANS 6:13 *And do not go on presenting the members of your body to sin as instruments of unrighteousness; but present yourselves to God as those alive from the dead, and your members as instruments of righteousness to God.*

—68—

FAKE IDS DON'T WORK

I know how easy it is to lose sight of your identity and begin to define yourself based on what you do. This hit home for me during the pandemic lockdown when churches shuttered their doors. The church I had pastored for more than four decades closed its doors, and preaching from the pulpit didn't take place for a number of months; when it resumed, at first it was to an empty church. It was a quite challenging time for me when so much of what I had done the previous forty years was tied to preaching there.

Men, in particular, define themselves by what they do. You see this whenever two men meet, and one of the first questions asked is about what they do. But we are much more than what we do. We are to be defined by our unique identity in Jesus Christ. How Jesus created you and the purpose He has for you ought to be your defining factors. Overcoming spiritual battles won't happen if you are living with a fake ID. Only a valid identity carries the spiritual weight and authority to defeat Satan. It's a hard lesson we all must learn. But in learning it, we discover the power to victoriously wage spiritual battle.

GALATIANS 2:20 *I have been crucified with Christ; and it is no longer I who live, but Christ lives in me; and the life which I now live in the flesh I live by faith in the Son of God, who loved me and gave Himself up for me.*

—69—

THE MYSTERY OF THE WORD

Many people give up reading the Bible because they don't understand it. But that is the best reason to keep reading it. You need to continue to read and study the Bible until you do understand it. Jesus often said when He taught, "He who has ears to hear, let him hear," which means that not everyone has been given the gift of understanding. That often comes through prayer, seeking the Lord, and reading the Bible. What's more, Scripture can work deep within you even when you don't understand it.

Hebrews 4:12 gives us insight into how God's Word works: "For the word of God is living and active and sharper than any two-edged sword, and piercing as far as the division of soul and spirit, of both joints and marrow, and able to judge the thoughts and intentions of the heart." In short, it is alive and able to penetrate areas of your understanding beyond the rational mind, reaching deep into the intentions of your heart.

Living by faith means not always understanding ahead of time what God is asking you to do. Keep reading and studying the Word until the Holy Spirit enables you to grasp it. Don't give up when concepts seem too challenging. Simply dig deeper and pray purely for the gift of understanding this mystery known as God's transforming Word.

JOHN 14:26 *But the Helper, the Holy Spirit, whom the Father will send in My name, He will teach you all things, and bring to your remembrance all that I said to you.*

—70—

A PARTITION PROBLEM

Home improvement experts are all about tearing down walls to make living spaces more open. The open floor plan has become very popular over the years as it transforms older homes into ones that seem contemporary. Tearing down walls to provide for greater usability of space is a great idea.

A lot of churches have classrooms with a partition down the middle that can be opened or closed. If the group meeting there wants to have two classes in the same space, they simply close the partition. They divide the room so information in one part of the room doesn't cross over to the other part, setting up silos of information within an existing space.

Satan also likes to set up dividers in our brains, creating divisions in our minds so we can wind up thinking two or more ways at the same time. Satan doesn't mind if you hear God's Word on Sunday morning, as long as in the other room of your mind you have Satan's thoughts on Monday (or even Sunday afternoon). The reason we stay defeated for so long in spiritual battles is due to partitions in the mind. When we live with partitions (or fortresses, as the Bible calls them), the truth of God can't get through. The enemy is able to keep the truth of God from fully infiltrating your thought patterns so you might have victory one moment but defeat in the next.

JAMES 4:8 *Draw near to God and He will draw near to you. Cleanse your hands, you sinners; and purify your hearts, you double-minded.*

—71—

FAITH EXPERTS

While the rich often have more *resources*, the poor often have more *faith*. Of course this is not always the case, but it tends to hold true. One reason is because God has often chosen people who don't have much by way of material possessions to be those who possess much faith. This faith grows and develops in them by virtue of difficulties and challenges. As they look to God for each need of theirs to be met, and even their wants, their faith increases as they see Him provide.

When you look to your bank account, job, inheritance, or investments as your source, you forget that it is God who is your Source. You might not feel that faith is necessary when you have access to all you need, and even want. But you'll soon discover when you face a health crisis or other personal crisis that faith in God is ultra important.

In order to know you can trust God, you need to trust God. You need to see His provision in your life in everyday ways. That's how you strengthen your faith muscles. Without faith, it is impossible to please God (Hebrews 11:6). It is also impossible to wage victorious spiritual warfare. Even if you have been blessed with material wealth, intentionally look for ways to depend on God. Don't allow your faith muscles to atrophy due to lack of use. That will only make you an easy target for the enemy.

MARK 11:22 *And Jesus answered saying to them, "Have faith in God."*

—72—

DIVINE DISRUPTION

God promises us peace. But the peace He promises to supply is on the inside. Nowhere in Scripture does God promise us peaceful situations in life. Nor does He promise us peaceful scenarios on the job or in our relationships. In fact, Jesus specifically states that in this world, we will have troubles (John 16:33). But God does promise us a peace that can surpass not only our understanding but also our circumstances. Peace never means that you won't have problems. Peace means that the problems you face, and the spiritual battles you encounter, won't have the last word on your life and emotions.

If you've ever had to remodel anything, you know how messy it can be. Everything seems to get disrupted when you're remodeling because to make way for the new, a destruction of the old has to occur first. When God allows something to be destroyed or deconstructed in your life, it might be because it has become stale and old. It may be an ineffective part of your life. It may also be a weak point where the enemy can attack. Thus, God will often allow difficulties in order to develop you. These disruptions are designed to help you look at your life and assess where you are in your spiritual walk. A "form of godliness" will get you nowhere on the spiritual battlefield. It is only true kingdom authority that conquers the evil one.

2 TIMOTHY 3:5 *Holding to a form of godliness, although they have denied its power; Avoid such men as these.*

—73—

RELIGION WITHOUT JESUS

While religion has always been about following the rules, Christianity is (or should be) different altogether. Christianity is different from all other religions because Jesus came to bring us something new—a new covenant. Jesus didn't come to earth merely to fix an old system. He offers us a relationship with God himself.

Religion, without Jesus, can turn you into a depressed slave. Religion can actually hold you hostage. Legalism, especially, can make a person miserable. When all you do is focus on the dos and the don'ts of attempting to appease God, you will find yourself forever chasing a goal you cannot reach. Sure, you might be serving God, but you'll be serving Him without a smile because it takes all your effort to keep up with all the regulations and rules. What's worse is that oftentimes those in charge of religious groups add new stuff for you to live up to. It becomes a never-ending barrage of religiosity.

Jesus told us that no one puts new wine into old wineskins. What He meant is that He had created something new. He didn't come to reform religion. Jesus came to offer a new way, rooted in a relationship with Him. Satan wants to keep you thinking that religion will save you. But only the blood of Jesus Christ saves. When you embrace that new mindset, the chains of religion drop off you.

EPHESIANS 1:7 *In Him we have redemption through His blood, the forgiveness of our trespasses, according to the riches of His grace.*

—74—

JESUS AND . . .

Some things are better mixed together. Take peanut butter and jelly. Peanut butter by itself can get very bland, and sticky. But adding jelly to it makes a perfect combination for a sandwich. Soap on its own won't do you much good, but when you combine it with water, you have an effective means of cleaning up. I think you get the idea. But the greater point I want to make is that while many things are better mixed together, there is one thing that is perfect standing on its own: salvation in Jesus Christ.

You can't trust in Jesus Christ for your salvation but then mix your faith with your act of baptism. Neither can you mix your faith with your church membership or good works. You can't even mix your faith with your tithes or giving. It is faith alone in Christ alone that supplies you with salvation, giving you the gift of eternal life.

A devotion a day doesn't keep the devil away. But the devil would love for you to believe that. If Satan can confuse you into thinking that your spiritual authority is rooted in your own righteousness and acts of devotion to God, then Satan will have you beat. Your authority as you wage spiritual warfare is rooted in the shed blood of Jesus Christ.

1 JOHN 1:7 *But if we walk in the Light as He Himself is in the Light, we have fellowship with one another, and the blood of Jesus His Son cleanses us from all sin.*

— 75 —

UNHEALTHY RELIGION

It's critical to truly distinguish between religion and your relationship with Jesus Christ because religion is one of the traps Satan uses to dull people to the Lord. Satan can also hinder people's participation in spiritual warfare by getting them too focused on religion and religious activity. A person's social circle can often tell you a lot about him or her. When Jesus spent time on earth, He spent a lot of His time with publicans and sinners. That says a lot about how He views them. The publicans and sinners proved to be more responsive to Him than those who were steeped in the traditions of religion.

Religion without Jesus is like putting muscle pain-relief cream on a broken leg: It might make you feel better for a moment, but you haven't fixed a thing. When your soul and relationship with God are broken due to sin, you need more than religion to fix the situation. You need more than good works to fix it. You need more than money to fix it. You need the atoning sacrifice of the Lord Jesus Christ. Understanding and embracing that reality, and fully living in that truth, is what it means to wear the helmet of salvation that enables you to fight spiritual battles well.

ROMANS 3:25 *Whom God displayed publicly as a propitiation in His blood through faith. This was to demonstrate His righteousness, because in the forbearance of God He passed over the sins previously committed.*

—76—

RULES OR RELATIONSHIP

If Christianity isn't about following religious rules, then do the rules still matter? Yes, following God and striving to live according to His righteous standards matters. When you serve God out of love for Him, you will want to live according to His standard. Remember the Hebrews 4:12 insight that the Word of God is able to tell even the intentions of our heart. God wants to see what your intentions are for keeping the rules too. Many people view rule-following as a trade-off for blessings, or at least as a way to avoid trouble. But God wants His righteous standard followed out of a heart of love.

There was a woman who was married to a man who didn't love her but had a lot of rules. He just wanted help around the house. After her husband died, she married another man whom she loved, and he loved her. The woman found the list from her first husband in a dresser drawer and was surprised to discover that she was keeping all of his rules that had caused her so much grief before. With her current husband she did the tasks easily, all because she was serving him out of love.

God desires that you serve Him out of love. You'll tap into His kingdom authority and His covering in your life when you do that.

JOHN 15:4 *Abide in Me, and I in you. As the branch cannot bear fruit of itself unless it abides in the vine, so neither can you unless you abide in Me.*

— 77 —

OUR AUTHORITY OVER SATAN

As we addressed in an early devotional, Satan is a defeated enemy, but still powerful. It takes spiritual *authority* to beat Satan, and the way to access that is through Jesus Christ. Your relationship with Jesus is the central component in fighting the good fight.

Ephesians 1:18–23 says,

> I pray that the eyes of your heart may be enlightened, so that you will know what is the hope of His calling, what are the riches of the glory of His inheritance in the saints, and what is the surpassing greatness of His power toward us who believe. These are in accordance with the working of the strength of His might which He brought about in Christ, when He raised Him from the dead and seated Him at His right hand in the heavenly places, far above all rule and authority and power and dominion, and every name that is named, not only in this age but also in the one to come. And He put all things in subjection under His feet, and gave Him as head over all things to the church, which is His body, the fullness of Him who fills all in all.

As long as you are connected to Jesus Christ in relational harmony, you have access to His kingdom authority. To have spiritual authority, you must first be under spiritual authority.

JOHN 15:6 *If anyone does not abide in Me, he is thrown away as a branch and dries up; and they gather them, and cast them into the fire and they are burned.*

—78—

THE CHURCH BEING THE CHURCH

For men to gain insight into how to fight the good fight and overcome the enemy's schemes in their lives, they need to be surrounded by like-minded believers in the local church. But far too many churches are not being what the Bible has called them to be, which leads to men floundering in their roles and losing their battles.

The church has been delegated spiritual authority by Jesus Christ. "And coming to Him as to a living stone which has been rejected by men, but is choice and precious in the sight of God, you also, as living stones, are being built up as a spiritual house for a holy priesthood, to offer up spiritual sacrifices acceptable to God through Jesus Christ" (1 Peter 2:4–5). God chose to build a community of believers that was to function with such spiritual finesse, victory, and authority that even the gates of hell would not prevail against it. A church building will not stop the gates of hell from impacting our community and culture for evil. But a church can, if and when the church functions as a community of believers under the lordship of Jesus Christ.

Your battle is not your own. You are fighting within a community of believers God has equipped with the spiritual authority necessary to advance His kingdom agenda on earth.

MATTHEW 16:18 *I also say to you that you are Peter, and upon this rock I will build My church; and the gates of Hades will not overpower it.*

—79—

SATAN'S AGENDA FOR YOUR LIFE

Demons have one major goal: to trip you up. They watch you get up in the morning and start their attack on you before your feet even hit the floor. Sometimes they use your friends, family, or coworkers. Other times they use your own thoughts against you. Their strategy is to get you fixated on anything other than Jesus Christ.

If you are seeking to live for Jesus Christ, you need to be aware of the demons' approach in your life. You need to evaluate your own weak areas so you can strengthen them. What's more, if you falter or fail, look to the cross of Jesus Christ that offers forgiveness and restoration. One way Satan sidelines so many saints is through a misuse of guilt and shame. What Jesus has forgiven and paid for on the cross, you do not need to pay for again through personal shame or punishment. Accept Christ's forgiveness and move forward. The longer Satan can keep you sidelined from making a kingdom impact, the longer he holds the high ground in this spiritual battle.

Satan's schemes are targeted and he seeks to exploit your weaknesses, so live with a mindset of awareness toward his tactics. Do not be caught off guard.

1 CORINTHIANS 10:13 *No temptation has overtaken you but such as is common to man; and God is faithful, who will not allow you to be tempted beyond what you are able, but with the temptation will provide the way of escape also, so that you will be able to endure it.*

Kingdom authority comes from the Spirit within when your spirit operates in alignment under the lordship of Jesus Christ.

— 80 —

GETTING OUR RIGHTS ALL WRONG

Most of us have been taught to value individuality, independence, and freedom, and we should. These are good values. However, if we want to gain access to victory in spiritual warfare, we need to understand how to first surrender to a higher authority—Jesus. When victory is to be ours, it is only because victory is His. When it comes to your spiritual life, the wrong kind of independence can be deadly.

One of the major issues in Christianity today is that too many believers feel they are in charge of their lives. But if you are in charge of your own life, you can't be a vital part of God's kingdom battle plan. If you are running your own agenda, you won't be a part of God's greater kingdom agenda.

My favorite verse is Galatians 2:20. It summarizes the aim of the Christian life: "I have been crucified with Christ; and it is no longer I who live, but Christ lives in me; and the life which I now live in the flesh I live by faith in the Son of God, who loved me and gave Himself up for me." Kingdom authority does not exist in your plans, your goals, your determination, or even in your positive thinking. Kingdom authority comes from the Spirit within when your spirit operates in alignment under the lordship of Jesus Christ.

JOHN 15:14 *You are My friends if you do what I command you.*

—81—

USING YOUR SPIRITUAL AUTHORITY

Authority always demands responsibility. Kingdom authority requires spiritual responsibility too. God does not grow us up and mature us so that He will have to continue bailing us out. He matures us so that we will live with spiritual responsibility. Let me show you what I mean by looking at Exodus 14:13. It says, "But Moses said to the people, 'Do not fear! Stand by and see the salvation of the LORD which He will accomplish for you today; for the Egyptians whom you have seen today, you will never see them again forever.'" In other words, a miracle was about to happen. And yet in verse 15, we discover they did not act on the promise of this miracle.

We read in Exodus 14:15, "Then the LORD said to Moses, 'Why are you crying out to Me? Tell the sons of Israel to go forward.'" God was ready to perform His miracle. He had even told them to stand by and see the salvation of the Lord. Yet a couple of verses later, we see that He is waiting on them to move. Praising God is not enough for fighting the good fight. Honoring God is not enough. Even believing God is not enough. There are occasions in life where you must move. Often, in fact, He asks you to do something to demonstrate your faith. That's when you experience your miracles.

LUKE 17:5 *The apostles said to the Lord, "Increase our faith!"*

— 82 —

IT COMES WITH THE TERRITORY

Before you start reading the Bible, I encourage you to read Ephesians 1:18, and even memorize it: "I pray that the eyes of your heart may be enlightened, so that you will know what is the hope of His calling, what are the riches of the glory of His inheritance in the saints." You can turn this verse into a prayer before reading Scripture, praying, "Lord Jesus, open the eyes of my heart so that I will be enlightened to know the hope of Your calling for my life, and for those I love."

It is important to discern God's will for your life so you can intentionally follow Him and His guidance. One way this discernment is given is through prayer and reading the Word. Because Jesus is seated above all authority, power, dominion, and every name that is to be named in this age and the age to come, He has His foot on the neck of your enemies. Jesus is in charge. Your goal ought to be discovering what Jesus wants done in and through your life. Once you do, you will flow more freely in your assignments because you will have tapped into Christ's kingdom authority.

We sometimes forget how powerful Jesus is, partly due to our culture's marginalization of Him. But don't fall prey to a lesser view of Jesus Christ. Jesus is all you need to wage victorious warfare.

PSALM 110:1 *The Lord says to my Lord: "Sit at My right hand until I make Your enemies a footstool for Your feet."*

83

KEEP THE RECEIPT

With every purchase, you should get a receipt that verifies you paid for the item you received. When Jesus Christ died on the cross for our sins, the debt we owed was paid in full. Jesus' resurrection is our receipt, our proof that our sin debt was paid in full. That's why Jesus didn't rise privately; 1 Corinthians 15 tells us He was seen by more than 500 brethren. Jesus' public resurrection demonstrates that you no longer owe God your sin debt. That should give you greater confidence in facing the enemy.

Romans 8:1 declares, "Therefore there is now no condemnation for those who are in Christ Jesus." The receipt of the resurrection has removed any condemnation you or I once had. Jesus is the conqueror, seated at the right hand of the Father and able to deliver us not only from sin itself, but from the consequences as well—when we confess and repent of what we have done. Satan loves to try to hold people hostage for sins they committed in the past, or strongholds and sins presently trapping them. But the receipt of Jesus Christ declares the sin debt paid. You do not owe any more shame or any more guilt. You do not owe Him good deeds. Your service to God should be done out of a heart of gratitude. Wear your helmet of salvation without shame because Jesus has paid the price in full.

1 CORINTHIANS 2:5 *So that your faith would not rest on the wisdom of men, but on the power of God.*

—84—

BELIEVING A LIE

Where does a powerless enemy get his power? Too often, he gets it from *us*—from our own doubts, fears, sin, and shame. Hebrews 2:14 tells us that Satan was rendered powerless: "Therefore, since the children share in flesh and blood, He Himself likewise also partook of the same, that through death He might render powerless him who had the power of death, that is, the devil." And while the passage refers to the power of death, it reminds us that Satan's spiritual authority was stripped at the cross. He has no authority over us.

Satan and his demons have no more claim on you than what you give them. When you trusted in Jesus for salvation, you were saved not only for eternity but also on earth—saved from Satan's grip. But too often we not only fail to wage spiritual warfare well, we also help the enemy. We bulk up the enemy through wrong choices, thoughts, and actions. We are to make it a point to remain humble, give God thanks, and live a righteous life before the Lord. When you do fail, come to His throne for forgiveness and restoration. Don't feed the enemy in this battle.

JOHN 8:44 *You are of your father the devil, and you want to do the desires of your father. He was a murderer from the beginning, and does not stand in the truth because there is no truth in him. Whenever he speaks a lie, he speaks from his own nature, for he is a liar and the father of lies.*

85

ACTIVATING ANGELS

If you've been waiting for some heavenly help with your earthly problems, you should know that those heavenly helpers might be waiting on you. You and I were created a little lower than the angels, but when Jesus Christ rose from the dead, we were given platform shoes. These shoes have a raised sole that gives the wearer extra height. So we are enabled to activate angels on our behalf when we do it according to the power and name of Jesus Christ. Even though angels are higher than us in the spiritual hierarchy, we have direct access to Jesus and can call upon them for help.

Your angels often will not move on your behalf until they see you move in faith. They watch to see if you are following Jesus and tapping into His spiritual authority. The angels follow Jesus' lead. When they see you living in a manner consistent with the kingdom of God, that sets them free to work on your behalf. Many of us don't get angelic help in our spiritual battles simply because we don't understand that the angels are waiting on us to respond to God first. They are waiting for us to demonstrate true faith and love. When you do that, you gain access to an angelic realm able to battle the demons on your behalf.

MATTHEW 18:10 *See that you do not despise one of these little ones, for I say to you that their angels in heaven continually see the face of My Father who is in heaven.*

— 86 —

IT TAKES A COMMUNITY

We come to Christ as individuals, but growth often takes place in the presence of community. That's why attending church is so important. That's why taking part in Bible studies is too, as well as relationships and accountability. We grow in our spiritual walk as "iron sharpens iron" (Proverbs 27:17) and we disciple one another. Jesus came to establish the church and build His community of saints. He didn't come so believers would live isolated lives. How effective would a military be at fighting off the enemy if soldiers all operated independently of one another?

God has ordained the church as an entity that can stop the gates of hell from advancing on His kingdom. But that is only when the church is functioning as a community of believers in connection to His revealed will and under His rule and authority.

Instead of focusing all your time and efforts on the evil one and his demons, start taking a closer look at what Jesus is doing, and wants to do, through your connection to a community of believers. Start studying Jesus' battle plan, then join up with others who are studying it too. That's the difference between living a life on the offensive instead of on the defensive. Jesus came to build His church to advance. He came that we may live on the offensive and advance His kingdom agenda on earth.

1 PETER 2:5 *You also, as living stones, are being built up as a spiritual house for a holy priesthood, to offer up spiritual sacrifices acceptable to God through Jesus Christ.*

— 87 —

FIGHTING THE WRONG FIGHT

It doesn't matter how well the battle is going if you are fighting the wrong enemy. That's why so many of us have a hard time standing firm in our faith. Believers are to be equipped with the armor of God. We are told in Ephesians 6:11 why we are given this: "Put on the full armor of God, so that you will be able to stand firm against the schemes of the devil." The enemy we are standing firm against is the devil. Satan would love for you to forget that!

Satan aims to deceive each of us into thinking we are fighting people, circumstances, or even ourselves. But we do not fight against flesh and blood. That is not the right battle. We fight against Satan and his demons. Thus, it's important to fight using the armor of God and not human tools. You must use the armor of God to fight the good fight. If you rely on your own cleverness, abilities, or strategy, you will lose every time. Spiritual warfare is only won through the use of spiritual weapons.

Identifying your true enemy is step one. When someone or something irritates you, trips you up, or tempts you, pray and ask God to reveal what the enemy is up to. Ask for wisdom to face the situation at hand. Looking to God for His wisdom is a positive step in preparing you for fighting spiritual warfare well.

EPHESIANS 6:23 *Peace be to the brethren, and love with faith, from God the Father and the Lord Jesus Christ.*

—88—

THE FINAL WORD

With the advent of social media years ago, the ability and opportunity for people—even strangers—to discuss various topics exploded. There's always someone somewhere to respond and engage if you look hard enough, or post frequently enough. But when it comes down to it, there's only one opinion that matters, no matter the subject.

Hebrews 1:1–3 tells us where we should get our authoritative information and answers: "God, after He spoke long ago to the fathers in the prophets in many portions and in many ways, in these last days has spoken to us in His Son, whom He appointed heir of all things, through whom also He made the world. And He is the radiance of His glory and the exact representation of His nature, and upholds all things by the word of His power."

Jesus Christ is the final word on all things, including how you approach your home, career, finances, relationships, community life, and everything else. That is why Hebrews 12:25 tells us, "See to it that you do not refuse Him who is speaking. For if those did not escape when they refused him who warned them on earth, much less will we escape who turn away from Him who warns from heaven." Unless and until you listen to Jesus and let Him be your sole guide, you may discover some shaking in your life.

HEBREWS 12:28 *Therefore, since we receive a kingdom which cannot be shaken, let us show gratitude, by which we may offer to God an acceptable service with reverence and awe.*

—89—

WHEN ALL HELL BREAKS LOOSE

Ephesians 6:13 lets us know that some days are better than others. "Therefore, take up the full armor of God, so that you will be able to resist in the evil day, and having done everything, to stand firm." The "evil day" in this verse is the day when your number comes up. It refers to when Satan chooses to unleash hell after you. If you are in a peaceful season right now, I encourage you to enjoy it because tomorrow may be the evil day.

If we look at Job, we are reminded how quickly things can go south. Job lived a very profitable and comfortable life. He had a large family and had achieved much worldly success. Yet when Satan called Job's number, God allowed it (up to a certain extent). Things turned topsy-turvy in a minute. And you, like Job, need to stand firm when they do.

At the end of it all, Job kept his faith. He kept his hope in the goodness of God. He did not turn his back on the Lord. In fact, he said that even if God slew him, he would still praise Him. What Job was indicating is that even though he did not understand why everything had gone wrong, he still knew in his heart that God was good. When you don't trust God's hand, always trust His heart. That's how you'll stand firm in the evil day.

JOB 13:15 *Though He slay me, I will hope in Him. Nevertheless I will argue my ways before Him.*

— 90 —

DRESS FOR SPIRITUAL SUCCESS

Why do trials and temptations catch us by surprise? It's often the result of a spiritual wardrobe malfunction. Just as you must dress your body before heading out your door each day, you also must dress spiritually to fight the good fight. If you only grab the shield of faith, you will be underdressed. You wouldn't head to work in a pair of shorts, would you? There is a certain standard for clothing. Similarly, there exists a standard for dress when it comes to spiritual warfare. You must put on all of the armor of God, not just some of it.

Romans 13:11 reminds us that we are waking up: "Do this, knowing the time, that it is already the hour for you to awaken from sleep; for now salvation is nearer to us than when we believed." And what do you do when you wake up? You get dressed. Unfortunately, we have a lot of Christians who wake up from their sleep only to roll over and go back to bed. The problems arise because of a lack of initiative when facing the enemy. You can't wage victorious spiritual warfare in your pajamas in bed. You have to put on your Sunday best every day—every hour—that is, the armor of God. When you do that, you will be dressed for spiritual success.

ROMANS 13:12 *The night is almost gone, and the day is near. Therefore let us lay aside the deeds of darkness and put on the armor of light.*

—91—

STAYING WELL-DRESSED

Ephesians 6:11 describes the armor of God as a set of survival gear for Christians facing spiritual warfare. But did you know there is a subtle difference between some of our gear? The first three pieces of armor are written about with a verbal tense translated as "having," indicating a continuous state, meaning we have put them on and still have them on: "Stand firm therefore, having girded your loins with truth, and having put on the breastplate of righteousness" (v. 14). But when Paul gets to the last three pieces of armor, he shifts to verbs meaning to take: "in addition to all, taking up the shield of faith" (v. 16). Thus, while you are to have all your armor on at all times, the last three pieces you activate when you face a specific attack "in the evil day" (v. 13).

Understanding this distinction is important in knowing how to use the various pieces of armor. For example, if you purchased a tool or piece of equipment, you would read the manual on how to use it. You wouldn't make the financial investment in something designed to help you without also investing the time to understand how to use it. If you had a kerosene lantern with you in the woods at night but didn't know how to use it, it would still be dark all around you. You must understand how to use each piece of the armor for it to be effective.

EPHESIANS 6:24 *Grace be with all those who love our Lord Jesus Christ with incorruptible love.*

—92—

THE BATTLE IS THE LORD'S

The most important thing to know about the spiritual warfare we face as believers is that we *can't win*—not on our own. Satan would love for you to think that you can beat him yourself. You cannot win a battle against Satan. Neither can I. But the good news is we don't need to. God has established a way for us to team up with the Lord Jesus Christ, as well as His command of the angels, to defeat Satan and the demons. Ephesians 6:10 gives us insight: "Finally, be strong in the Lord and in the strength of His might."

Notice that you are to be strong "in the Lord," meaning the battle is not yours. The battle is the Lord's. The armor is God's armor. The warfare is God's work. To put it another way, you are to find your victory in Christ alone. It is in the strength of His might that you are made strong.

If you believe you are able to defeat Satan without relying on the Lord and His strength, might, and kingdom authority, you will set yourself up for defeat. But when you come at Satan in the name of the Lord Jesus Christ, you find strength that is greater than yours—and greater than the enemy's as well.

1 SAMUEL 17:47 *And that all this assembly may know that the Lord does not deliver by sword or by spear; for the battle is the Lord's and He will give you into our hands.*

—93—

IT STARTS WITH THE TRUTH

The Bible tells us to put on the *whole* armor of God if we want to stand firm in the face of spiritual warfare. That list of items in Ephesians 6 starts with a very important, and often overlooked, piece: truth. If you are going to dress up in Jesus, you are going to need a belt on. The belt that holds everything up and together is truth. Now, in the culture and days that Ephesians was written, there were Roman soldiers who wore long tunics that flowed down to the ground. But when it came time for a fight, a soldier couldn't really maneuver with that long tunic, so he would tuck it up under his belt.

The belt had loops on it to carry his sword and to connect his breastplate to it. It was the fundamental piece because everything connected to it or hung on it. If the Roman soldier didn't have his belt, he also couldn't wear his breastplate. If he didn't have his belt, he also couldn't carry his sword. If he didn't have his belt, he also couldn't hold everything together. In short, the soldier couldn't stand firm.

When Satan seeks to steal your joy, family, identity, purpose, or peace, be sure to stand firm. You stand firm first and foremost by being rooted in the truth of God's character, attributes, and Word. And you must know the character, attributes, and Word of God to live rooted in them.

PSALM 50:6 *And the heavens declare His righteousness, for God Himself is judge. Selah.*

—94—

WHO DECIDES WHAT'S WHAT?

Our society keeps trying to reduce truth to nothing more than a matter of opinion. It's a strategy Satan has employed throughout time, starting with Eve in the garden. The first thing Satan did was try to get Eve to question what God said, to plant doubts in her mind. And he's been doing it ever since.

People want objective standards of truth when it comes to a lot of things in life, but when it comes to what God says, they want to leave it up to everyone's thoughts on the matter. For example, suppose you got on an airplane and the pilot said over the loudspeaker, "I think I feel like pushing this button today instead—just to see how it works." Or what if you went to the doctor and he said he learned how to do the surgery in school but he wanted to try something new he had read online? Would you stay on that plane or have the surgery done by that doctor? Probably not, and neither would I.

Objective standards of truth are important. Since God created this world, He gets to decide what's what. After all, it is God's standard of truth known as physics that holds the world together. Waging spiritual warfare without truth is like trying to fish without a line, net, or spear. You'll be there all night, and never catch a thing.

JOHN 14:6 *Jesus said to him, "I am the way, and the truth, and the life; no one comes to the Father but through Me."*

— 95 —

THE NARROW WAY

Have you ever worn a belt that felt uncomfortable? Maybe it was too tight or it pinched in your clothes too much. The belt of truth in the armor of God can feel uncomfortable at times too. It might feel too restricting. But the reason belts exist is to keep things in place. Uncomfortable or not, you are saving yourself from a very embarrassing situation when you keep your belt on.

John 14:6 says, "Jesus said to him, 'I am the way, and the truth, and the life; no one comes to the Father but through Me.'" Jesus is the truth. Truth is not only a concept. Truth is a person. Truth includes the written Word of God as well as the living Word of God. To live with the belt of truth on means you are abiding in Jesus Christ. He knows the mind of the Father and can disclose truth to you through the presence of the Holy Spirit.

Your close relationship with Jesus Christ gives you strength, peace, and the wisdom to fight the good fight against the enemy's schemes. That may mean you feel uncomfortable in some social situations, or your lifestyle may wind up more restricted than you hoped—but Jesus is there to hold you together.

1 JOHN 5:20 *And we know that the Son of God has come, and has given us understanding so that we may know Him who is true; and we are in Him who is true, in His Son Jesus Christ. This is the true God and eternal life.*

—96—

GOD IS YOUR SOURCE

If you think that the cash in your wallet comes from your job or that your health comes from good eating and exercise, you've missed something. God is your source. He is your only source.

Your job is not your source. Your bank is not your source. Your employer is not your source. Your spouse is not your source. God is your only source; everything else is a resource.

A tactic God uses, and one you must free Him up to use in spiritual warfare, is providing through a variety of ways. He can use whatever resource He wants to use, even if His supply comes through something you wouldn't normally think it would. Just because God is providing today through one channel doesn't mean He won't provide tomorrow through another. Sometimes things dry up. Economies dry up. Income dries up. The stocks go down. But when God allows things to dry up in your life, it is because He has a different plan. Maybe that plan involves reminding you that other things are not your source—God alone provides for you.

You don't need to give in to the devil's temptation in spiritual warfare to worry when things go wrong. Remember who your source is and you will continue to walk in faith and with peace.

2 CORINTHIANS 9:8 *And God is able to make all grace abound to you, so that always having all sufficiency in everything, you may have an abundance for every good deed.*

97

DOES GOD WANT YOUR MONEY?

Too many people miss out on Jesus because they think church is all about the offering. They stay away from church because they either feel guilty for not tithing or get annoyed that a tithe or offering is collected each week. But think about how that logic plays out in other places. When you go to the grocery store, do you tell the grocer that all he wants is your money? You typically don't, because you are getting something you need in exchange for your money, so it doesn't bother you to pay for it.

The question you need to ask, then, is what do you gain from attending church? God has set up the church as a body of believers to enable you to find community. This community should be providing you with a place to grow spiritually. It should also be providing you with fellowship and opportunities for outreach. Attending church is not simply something to cross off on your to-do list. You are to benefit from attending church, and one of the ways you do that is by getting more involved. If you only attend on Sunday morning, you might not be gaining all the benefits God has for you through participating in church. God wants you to grow and develop spiritually so that you can fight the good fight well. One way you do that is through regular participation locally in the body of Christ.

1 CORINTHIANS 12:27 *Now you are Christ's body, and individually members of it.*

—98—

PRIMING THE PUMP

A man was lost in the desert one day, and it was blazing hot. He desperately needed to get to some water or he would soon die of thirst. He saw a shack ahead, and when he went inside, he found a pump connected to a well. The man began to pump as hard as he could, but nothing came out. He thought the well was dry.

The man was about to give up when he noticed on the side of the shack a tall glass of water. The sign next to the water said, "Use this water to prime the pump, and then fill it up again for the next traveler." This man scratched his head. He faced a dilemma. He felt like he was about to die from thirst and had finally found a glass of water. But the sign told him that if he poured the water down the pump instead of drinking it, he could get more water.

That's often how we view what God has given us. God wants us to invest our gifts, time, talents, and even our money into eternal goals. But we often want to use it all up right now. Priming the pump with the water required faith. Using our time, talents, and treasures for God requires faith too. But in faith is precisely how you fight the good fight. Keep your eyes on eternity and you'll lay up treasures in heaven.

1 CORINTHIANS 10:31 *Whether, then, you eat or drink or whatever you do, do all to the glory of God.*

—99—

BE A PROVIDER

God has given us the perfect assignment to keep us busy while we're waiting for Him to provide what we need. Understanding and fulfilling this assignment strengthens you for spiritual warfare. It makes you a stronger opponent as you face the enemy. This is because it simultaneously strengthens your faith and your abiding relationship with Jesus Christ.

The secret to receiving the provision from God that you need is for you to provide for someone else in need. When God sees that you are freely giving to others, He also freely gives to you. In other words, you cannot be a miracle receiver unless you are willing to also be a miracle dispenser. That's the problem with people who come to God and only want to be blessed, but don't ever want to be a blessing. They want a miracle, but they have no interest in helping anyone else. God is not interested in those who are only interested in themselves. God wants to bless others through you.

Luke 6:38 is the basis for this spiritual principle. It says, "Give, and it will be given to you. They will pour into your lap a good measure—pressed down, shaken together, and running over. For by your standard of measure it will be measured to you in return." We are to give first, and then look to God to provide.

PHILIPPIANS 4:19 *And my God will supply all your needs according to His riches in glory in Christ Jesus.*

—100—

WHEN PRAYER ISN'T ENOUGH

Saying "I'll pray for you" can be a sign of true caring. But it can also be a total cop-out. Everybody needs someone in their life who cares enough about them to pick up a burden when it's too heavy for them to carry. Everybody needs somebody in their life who loves them, cares for them, understands their pain, and who will bear their burdens with them. The great tragedy is when you don't have that someone, and when you refuse to be that someone for someone else.

We have two extremes today in God's kingdom. We have people who are struggling with God and who won't allow anybody in their circle to pick up their burden and help them through. And we've got Christians who are too selfish to be a burden-bearer for somebody else. You need somebody in your life who's not only willing to pray for you, but who's also willing to be part of the solution to the very problem they're praying for. And you need to be that for someone else too.

That's why the Bible says faith without works is dead. And dead faith will do nothing for you in spiritual battles. Live out your faith in your daily life and watch God win your battles for you.

LUKE 17:6 *And the Lord said, "If you had faith like a mustard seed, you would say to this mulberry tree, 'Be uprooted and be planted in the sea'; and it would obey you."*

—101—

NOUNS THAT CAN'T HELP YOU

Most people think idol worship is only practiced in primitive cultures. But if you understand what the term really means, you'll see that it's as common as can be. In fact, America is full of idols and idolatry. An idol is any unauthorized noun (person, place, or thing) to which you look to have needs met in your life. It's any unauthorized noun that you've placed at a higher level than God. In biblical times, idols didn't just sit there and decorate a stand. The idol was looked to as a divine provider.

In places around the world, people still worship the sun and the moon and the stars and the water and the trees. They are worshiping these things because they are hoping their worship brings something to them.

You and I don't worship those kinds of things, but we do worship American idols in our culture. We worship people, popularity, power, prestige, and possessions because we look to these things to meet emotional or physical needs. Anytime you look to an unauthorized noun in an unprescribed way as more important than God, you have just created an idol. Breaking the commandment of having no idols before God will limit how successful you can be in spiritual warfare.

EXODUS 20:4 *You shall not make for yourself an idol, or any likeness of what is in heaven above or on the earth beneath or in the water under the earth.*

—102—

PASSIVE WRATH

Every parent knows that letting children learn from their mistakes can sometimes be the toughest punishment of all. God knows it too. One of the reasons we are witnessing all this chaos around us—in our own lives, in our culture, and in our country—is because God often allows us to learn from our wrong choices. This is known as the passive wrath of God. There exists the active wrath of God, which we see in the Old Testament when fire and brimstone would come down from heaven. God demonstrated His judgment and His wrath in active ways throughout Old Testament history.

But thanks to the death of Jesus Christ, which has satisfied the just wrath of God, today we primarily deal with the passive wrath of God, when God simply moves out of the way and lets us experience the consequences of our choices. Romans 1 talks about this, saying that because the people no longer retained the knowledge of God, God turned them over and released them to the consequence of their choices. God loves us and has given us free will. We sometimes choose to disobey Him. That's when He lovingly allows us to learn, grow, and mature by experiencing the consequences. Don't resist the lessons God has for you. Learn, then apply what you have learned in order to serve Him better.

JOHN 3:36 *He who believes in the Son has eternal life; but he who does not obey the Son will not see life, but the wrath of God abides on him.*

103

STANDING FIRM

Natural-born peacekeepers don't want to disagree with anybody. But you need to draw the line somewhere. You can't agree with everyone all the time and be honoring the truth and God's standard. A politician was once asked, "Where do you stand on this issue?"

He replied, "Well, it's really simple. Some of my friends stand on it this way. Some of my friends stand on it that way. I just stand with my friends." Ultimately, he had no position. That might work for a politician, but it won't work for a committed follower of Jesus Christ seeking to topple the enemy in his own schemes. It ought to be clear what you stand for. It ought to be clear what you believe to be true. It ought to be clear that you are a believer in the Lord Jesus Christ and that you serve the God of the Bible.

Other people around the world are serving their version of god in an evil and violent way—and not apologizing for it. In fact, they are killing in the name of their god and doing so without apology. God wants to know that you have taken your stand and made your decision to stand with Him. When He sees you are serious, you will gain even greater access to all you need to wage victorious spiritual battle.

LUKE 9:23 *And He was saying to them all, "If anyone wishes to come after Me, he must deny himself, and take up his cross daily and follow Me."*

—104—

MIRACLES FOR ORDINARY PEOPLE

The Bible tells us about an important prophet named Elijah. We read about what he accomplished in the Old Testament. But what stands out to me is that this man who could do miraculous things as a result of his faith was an ordinary man. James 5:17 says, "Elijah was a man with a nature like ours, and he prayed earnestly that it would not rain, and it did not rain on the earth for three years and six months." While it doesn't use the word *ordinary*, it does state that Elijah was a man with a nature like ours. In other words, he had no unique powers. Yet because he was closely connected to God, he saw God do miracles through him.

If you want to wage spiritual warfare in a way that allows God to carry out His miracles through you, be an ordinary man. Don't think too highly of yourself. But do stay closely connected to God. That is the secret to spiritual success. Elijah modeled this for us. In fact, if you read about Elijah's life in Scripture, you'll see that he wrestled with his emotions at times. He felt lonely at times. He didn't consider himself to be a superhero prophet. Elijah was powerful because his connection to God was personal. You can live a powerful spiritual life as well if you choose to abide closely with Christ.

MALACHI 4:5 *Behold, I am going to send you Elijah the prophet before the coming of the great and terrible day of the* LORD.

—105—

HILLBILLY ROAD BUMPS

The harder you try to be all things to all people, the more likely you'll wind up being nothing to anyone at all. You have probably learned that the hard way. Or you might have witnessed that reality in someone else. But did you know that can be true in your spiritual life as well?

If you have driven through the country long enough, you may have discovered what is known as a hillbilly road bump. A hillbilly road bump is a dead armadillo in the middle of the road. Over a half million armadillos are killed every year on the roads of America. It's not uncommon to see one in the middle of the road. One of the reasons so many armadillos end up dead is because they don't try to get off the road quickly. They become content walking down the middle of the road. They might start out crossing the road but will turn and decide to remain on it. They just don't have the sense to get out of the middle of the road.

These days, there are a lot of hillbilly road-bump Christians. They come to church but stay in the middle between a kingdom worldview and a worldly one. They are middle-ground believers, trying to please God and others at the same time. But that's a recipe for disaster, and a setup for spiritual struggles in your life. God rewards those who are entirely committed to Him.

JAMES 1:8 *Being a double-minded man, unstable in all his ways.*

106

CONCRETE FAITH

A rock-solid faith gives us the foundation we need to stand up to life's challenges. So if you seem to be losing your footing, you might want to check the strength of your faith. For example, if you want to make concrete, you go and get a bag of cement. Then you mix the bag of cement with water. When it settles, it becomes concrete.

For many of us, God is not yet concrete. He's not a solid reality in our lives. He's merely a concept in our minds. That's because we have spiritual cement that hasn't gotten mixed so that it gets hard. Without being mixed, it is useless.

For many of us, who God is and what God says is an idea in our minds that has not yet formed into concrete in our lives by mixing belief with faith. Faith is simply acting like God is telling the truth. That's why the Bible calls it *walking* by faith and not talking by faith, or feeling by faith, or even thinking by faith. If you want a concrete manifestation of God, then what you *believe* about God must be mixed with what you *do* in response. When you do that, you are exercising faith so that God can now become concrete in your life and not a theory in your head.

HEBREWS 11:6 *And without faith it is impossible to please Him, for he who comes to God must believe that He is and that He is a rewarder of those who seek Him.*

—107—

CATCH ME, I'M JUMPING!

Trust comes more naturally to some people than to others. So what makes the difference? Maybe you've seen it with kids. Some kids trust more easily than others do. With all my grandkids and great-grandkids, I have seen different levels of trust. I'll ask one to jump off the platform at church into my arms and he or she will jump without thinking twice. Others will hesitate and then jump. Still others want to stay put on the platform. Trust varies within each of us. God knows how He made us and He desires that we all trust Him equally. For some of us, faith and trust might come more easily. But when God sees you trusting Him, when He knows you are among the group who struggle to trust, He gets all the more excited.

Just as I would become more excited when a grandchild who has been hesitant to trust eventually decides to jump, God knows the level of faith certain actions require, and He honors your faith for trusting Him. It might not feel natural to you to wage spiritual warfare. You might have hesitations or doubts. But when you do trust God and battle with His armor on, He will reward your faith as He sees you learn to trust Him.

JOHN 11:40 *Jesus said to her, "Did I not say to you that if you believe, you will see the glory of God?*

—108—

NOT GETTING EATEN

The downward spiral that destroys so many individuals and families can be stopped before it starts by doing what God has told us to do. I have done thousands of sessions of couples counseling, and the fighting between mates never ceases to alarm me. These couples are mad at each other all the time. And yet I'll see them come to church together on Sunday as if nothing is wrong—all the while displaying to everyone through a sour countenance that *everything* is wrong.

Genesis 4:7 explains sin's effect on us not only individually but in our relationships: "If you do well, will not your countenance be lifted up? And if you do not do well, sin is crouching at the door; and its desire is for you, but you must master it." Sin crouches at the door of our hearts and our relationships. When we master it and seek harmony and love in our relationships, our countenance is lifted. When we fail to master it, we open the door to anger, depression, fighting, and other relational issues. Giving in to sin, even in small ways, opens the door for greater disharmony in your life. It feeds on itself and then multiplies. Living a right life before God can help restore relational harmony and give you the tools you need to overcome Satan's attacks on you and your family.

ROMANS 6:23 *For the wages of sin is death, but the free gift of God is eternal life in Christ Jesus our Lord.*

—109—

THE WAY OF CAIN

It's popular these days to worship do-it-yourself deities, false gods that cause us to think we can take care of ourselves. The book of Jude speaks briefly on this. Verses 10–13 say,

> But these men revile the things which they do not understand; and the things which they know by instinct, like unreasoning animals, by these things they are destroyed. Woe to them! For they have gone the way of Cain, and for pay they have rushed headlong into the error of Balaam, and perished in the rebellion of Korah. These are the men who are hidden reefs in your love feasts when they feast with you without fear, caring for themselves; clouds without water, carried along by winds; autumn trees without fruit, doubly dead, uprooted; wild waves of the sea, casting up their own shame like foam; wandering stars, for whom the black darkness has been reserved forever.

Cain created a false religion by seeking to come to God as he pleased, not as God prescribed. God has prescribed only one way to come to Him: Jesus Christ. When we think our own works or anything we do enables us to come to God, we are following the ways of Cain. We will wind up wandering like Cain. No person is saved through works. It is only through Jesus that we find salvation, and victory over Satan. Victory comes through the shed blood of Jesus.

GENESIS 4:5 *But for Cain and for his offering He had no regard. So Cain became very angry and his countenance fell.*

— 110 —

MOTION DETECTORS

Far too many men want God to move first. They want to play follow the leader. And while following God is right and good, God will sometimes ask us to move first. This is because He wants to see whether we will step out in faith and obey Him.

A number of years ago, we installed motion-detection lighting in the sanctuary and adjacent rooms. We did so because people were leaving the lights on, and the electrical bill was very high. The new lighting enabled us to save thousands of dollars simply because the lights turn off automatically when no motion is detected.

Now, the power in and to the room didn't change. There remained the same level of power supplied. But that power was only accessed by movement. Similarly, God has the spiritual power you need to defeat the devil and his schemes in your life. But many times, you will only access this spiritual power through movement. God wants you to demonstrate your faith through your actions. He will often reward faith-based movement with a greater level of spiritual power and kingdom authority. You are to apply faith in every area of your life, which means you are to obey God in every area of your life. When you do that, your life will show movement in the direction of God's guiding Word.

MARK 9:23 *And Jesus said to him, "'If You can?' All things are possible to him who believes."*

— 111 —

CALLING GOD A LIAR

When you fail to act on faith, you are not only stuck with no help but your own, but you are also sending God a very dangerous message. Faith is not *one* of the things you need in your life and spiritual battles. Faith is the *key* thing you need if you want to experience God's overcoming power made manifest in spiritual warfare. If you choose to live a faithless life and just visit faith once in a while, you will not gain consistent victory in spiritual battles. This is because it takes faith to please God. To not live by faith is like calling God a liar.

Every time you choose to doubt what God has said or do not step out in faith, you demonstrate that you do not trust His integrity. You essentially tell God that He doesn't know what He is talking about. While nobody would come out and say that God is a liar, living without actions based on faith in His Word says the same thing. Why would God defend you against the enemy if you are siding with the enemy on what you believe to be true? Consider that the next time you face spiritual warfare, and let your actions reflect a heart that trusts in God.

NUMBERS 23:19 *God is not a man, that He should lie, nor a son of man, that He should repent; has He said, and will He not do it? Or has He spoken, and will He not make it good?*

—112—

WALKING ON THE ICE

When getting from point A to point B calls for a walk of faith, the decision doesn't really depend on what you think of the road, but rather what you think about God. Have you ever seen a pond during winter? If the temperature gets cold enough, it can freeze over. But just because it is frozen doesn't mean it is safe to walk across.

One time I was asked to walk across a lake to reach the other side of a camp. My concerns were high until I saw a truck drive across. Then I knew the ice was thick enough to hold me. My faith grew as I saw faith demonstrated by others. Similarly, we can encourage each other to walk by faith by living a life of faith ourselves. The Christian life isn't only about yourself. When you learn to fight the good fight and battle spiritual warfare with excellence, you can serve as a testimony to others. That doesn't mean you will live perfectly. None of us does. But when you fail, confession to God and accepting His forgiveness also demonstrates your faith. How many men sideline themselves after failure rather than taking the greater risk of faith to trust that Christ's redemptive power on the cross was enough to cover their sin? Let's be a testimony of how great God is rather than how great we are. That will inspire more people to walk by faith.

MATTHEW 21:22 *And all things you ask in prayer, believing, you will receive.*

— 113 —

WALKING WITH GOD

A lot of people who think they are walking with God are more out of step than they realize. To walk with God is to bring God to bear in the steps you take. It means God is part of your decision-making and thought processes. God is part of your calendar, your schedule, and your relationships. To walk with God means that you align with God as best you can every step you take and everything you're involved in.

If I told you I walked in the rain, I am explaining the atmosphere, or the environment, in which I walked. I walked in a wet environment because I walked in the rain. Similarly, to walk in the spirit, or to walk with God, is to walk so that God is controlling the environment of your movement. If God is not controlling the environment of your movement, except on Sunday morning, then you are not walking with God. When you learn how to walk with God regularly, you'll discover that battling the enemy comes more naturally to you because it is the Spirit at work in you waging the warfare on your behalf. Rather than focusing on the spiritual battle, try focusing on nurturing your walk with God and fellowshipping with the Spirit. When you do that, you will discover that He wages warfare on your behalf and you will experience victory in more areas of your life.

JOHN 15:7 *If you abide in Me, and My words abide in you, ask whatever you wish, and it will be done for you.*

—114—

BELIEVING WITHOUT SEEING

God wants a close, personal relationship with His people. He wants you to view Him as you would a friend or relative. Too many men view God as a boss or as a cosmic genie. But God's love for you goes deeper than that.

Jesus is not physically here on earth in the room where you can see Him. Similarly, God is spirit by nature. But this truth reminds me of the teacher who was an atheist and asked the kids in the class, "Can you see the trees?" And they said yes. Then the teacher asked, "Do you see the flowers?" And the kids again replied yes.

"What about the sun and the stars?" she asked. The kids responded yes. Then she thought she had them: "Can you see God?" The kids said no. So she told them God must not exist. But a boy raised his hand and asked, "Can you see your mind?" The teacher said no. The boy replied, "Does that mean you don't have one?" The teacher got the point.

We may not be able to see God physically, but we can see the physical manifestations of His presence and creativity every day. He desires to have a relationship with you as you have with someone you see. Such a relationship demonstrates faith—a belief not based on what you see. And faith is part of the armor of God.

JOHN 4:24 *God is spirit, and those who worship Him must worship in spirit and truth.*

—115—

IT'S ALL RUNNING DOWN

Your cell phone will eventually lose power if you don't plug it in to recharge. The same thing can happen to the universe. There is a law called the second law of thermodynamics, also known as entropy, which simply means the world is running down. You and I are also running down. We are getting older and grayer by the day. If the world is running down, though, that means it's not self-sustaining. So just like your house or your body, someone has to keep it up. That someone is God. Since God created the world, He knows how to regenerate it and sustain it. We witness His regenerating power all the time.

Living a life of spiritual victory means understanding that when things run down in your own life or spiritual walk, you need to look to the Creator to renew and regenerate you. Look to His Word. Seek His Spirit. Ask Him for His strength. It is God who is at work in you to sustain you. Never think that it is your own job to do so. That is the root of pride. It is God who is the source of your spiritual life and your spiritual victories in life. Look to Him.

REVELATION 21:5 *And He who sits on the throne said, "Behold, I am making all things new." And He said, "Write, for these words are faithful and true."*

— 116 —

MOVE THE STONE

The best evidence that we *believe* in God is that we *obey* Him. You remember the story in John 11 of Martha and Mary when Lazarus died and was put in the tomb? Jesus went to the tomb and told Martha to move the stone. Martha reminded Jesus that Lazarus had been dead four days and that by then, he would stink. Jesus had not asked Martha for instructions in mortuary science. He just told her to move the stone.

When God gives you an instruction, it might not make sense. In fact, it might seem to be the opposite of good sense. Oftentimes He will do that in order to give you an opportunity to demonstrate your faith. Faith is a critical component for fighting your battles well. When we don't have faith, Satan has the upper hand. Jesus identifies the level of your faith by your obedience to Him. When Martha agreed to have the stone removed, she experienced the miracle she desired. She experienced the resurrection of her brother, Lazarus.

If you need a miracle in your life, can you identify a call from God to obedience that you might not have followed through on yet? Pray for God to reveal His will for your life so that you can get in alignment with Him. Overcoming the enemy involves obedience to God, especially in those times that seem to make no sense at all.

JOHN 20:29 *Jesus said to him, "Because you have seen Me, have you believed? Blessed are they who did not see, and yet believed."*

—117—

WALKING IN AGREEMENT

If you are a walker and you walk with someone, it's probably somebody you like. You probably don't walk with someone you don't like because you're not in harmony with them. It would be an uncomfortable walk. Amos 3:3 states, "Do two men walk together unless they have made an appointment?" In other words, they need to agree to walk together in order to walk together.

To walk with God involves an agreement as well. First of all, it involves an agreement that you are going where He is going. Second, you agree to walk at His pace. You are also agreeing to hang out with Him. What's more, it presumes that you and He are getting along. It's a challenge to walk in step with someone you don't get along with.

Walking by faith with God involves a lot more than simply stepping out in faith. While that is good, God also desires a close relationship with you in such a way that you walk together with Him. You talk with Him. You laugh with Him. You carry on deep conversations with Him. You give Him time to respond to you. A lot can happen on a walk. Not only does it keep you physically fit, but it also strengthens your relationship with whomever you choose to walk alongside. A strong relationship with God will go far in spiritual warfare.

JAMES 1:6 *But he must ask in faith without any doubting, for the one who doubts is like the surf of the sea, driven and tossed by the wind.*

— 118 —

CLOSE ENOUGH TO HEAR GOD

God speaks to us in a number of ways. If you are not hearing Him, maybe it is because you have wandered out of earshot. Scripture tells us that Noah walked close to God. God was able to tell Noah about the upcoming destruction of the world because Noah was within earshot.

God wants to talk to you but He will only speak—He won't shout. When God spoke to Elijah in the desert, He didn't yell. He whispered. God will often whisper to us so that He knows we are truly listening. We live in a noise-cluttered world. Sounds surround us. Distractions call for our attention. But God wants us to train our ears to hear His voice because then we will be told things others may not hear.

If you were in a physical battle with someone in a boxing ring, wouldn't you want to hear your coach's voice? Even with the audience yelling and cheering, you would be able to do that because you would know how important his or her instructions would be. Similarly, as you wage spiritual warfare, you must attune your ears to the voice of the Lord. You can do it. It's just a matter of training.

1 Kings 19:13 *When Elijah heard it, he wrapped his face in his mantle and went out and stood in the entrance of the cave. And behold, a voice came to him and said, "What are you doing here, Elijah?"*

—119—

THROW THE NET

The Bible tells us that God's ways aren't our ways. "For My thoughts are not your thoughts, nor are your ways My ways," declares the LORD. "For as the heavens are higher than the earth, so are My ways higher than your ways and My thoughts than your thoughts" (Isaiah 55:8–9). A great example of this is when Peter was fishing, before he became a disciple. Jesus told Peter to cast his net on the other side of the boat. But Peter let Him know he had been fishing all night long and hadn't caught a thing.

Peter was a professional. He had probably been fishing since he was old enough to walk. For whatever reason, the fish weren't biting. Tossing the net to another part of the water wasn't going to change that. But Jesus encouraged Peter to give it a try. That's when Peter learned firsthand that God's ways are not our ways. As the Creator of the universe in which we live, God sees more than we could ever see.

It makes sense to listen to Him and trust Him, doing what He tells us to do. That's the most strategic, wise way to live life on earth. If you do, you'll see Him reveal ways to defeat the enemy that you had never dreamed possible.

ISAIAH 55:11 *So will My word be which goes forth from My mouth; it will not return to Me empty, without accomplishing what I desire, and without succeeding in the matter for which I sent it.*

—120—

MOVING AWAY FROM WORLDLINESS

If your Christian life isn't going anywhere spiritually with regard to waging victorious battles, it might be because you are too comfortable where you are. You will never know where God is taking you unless you are willing to leave where you are right now. Whether that relates to a career, home, dream, or whatever it is that brings you comfort and stability, God will often have more in store for you. But you might not get there if you choose to embrace your comfort more tightly than your Christian faith. God has a plan for you. Along the pathway of that plan you will face spiritual battles. But don't let those battles discourage you into retreating back to your comfort zone.

No growth related to faith ever happened in a comfort zone. Faith requires that you stretch your trust and belief muscles. When you do, God will show you where He wants to take you. He will show you a higher calling. He will reveal a plan and destiny for you that is more than you ever dreamed for yourself. When God created you, He created you with a kingdom purpose. But achieving this kingdom purpose can only happen if you are willing to leave your comfort zone, fight the good spiritual fight, and follow Christ.

1 JOHN 5:5 *Who is the one who overcomes the world, but he who believes that Jesus is the Son of God?*

—121—

STUCK IN A HOLDING PATTERN

As Christians, our ultimate destination is guaranteed. But the path God lays out to get us from here to there usually isn't the straight line we expected. I remember being on a flight and the pilot saying over the loudspeaker that there was bad weather around the city we were flying to. He said we would be entering into a holding pattern. Now, I had plans for a speaking engagement. The holding pattern caused a delay for me and for everyone on the plane. Some passengers needed to make a connecting flight. Nervousness crept onto our faces.

A spiritual holding pattern can mess with your plans as well. God will sometimes put you or me in a holding pattern when He is trying to either protect us from something negative up ahead or get our attention. But what is most important to remember is that God only does it because He has our best interest in mind. Just like the pilot didn't circle in a holding pattern to be cruel, God only pauses our plans and our life goals when He is looking out for us. Trust Him even when life isn't going according to your plans. This level of trust will honor Him and defeat Satan's attempts to create bitterness and doubt in your heart.

ECCLESIASTES 3:11 *He has made everything appropriate in its time. He has also set eternity in their heart, yet so that man will not find out the work which God has done from the beginning even to the end.*

—122—

USE THE POWER

God has unlimited power that He's more than willing to share with you. But too many Christians don't take Him up on His offer. It's possible that they are just too stuck on what they know and how things have always been.

There was an older lady living out in the country where electricity had never been run before. When the electrical company finally got around to supplying electricity to her area, she was thrilled. She would now have electricity for when it got dark. The electrical installation went well, but a few months later, the company noticed that the woman had barely used any of it. When they went to her home to find out why, she explained that she did use it every day. When it got dark at night, she would turn on the electricity so she could clearly see how to light her kerosene lamps. Then she would turn off the electricity.

See, she had power but she was stuck in her ways. She was stuck in all that she had known. She was trapped in a belief system—not in a power-shortage system. Similarly, you have all the kingdom authority you need to overcome the enemy's schemes in your life, but it will not do you any good until you start using it.

DEUTERONOMY 28:7 *The Lord shall cause your enemies who rise up against you to be defeated before you; they will come out against you one way and will flee before you seven ways.*

—123—

DON'T FIX IT

The saying goes, "If it ain't broke, don't fix it." But when it comes to your life, you should be careful not to try to fix it yourself even when it is broken. That's because there are some things that God wants us to grow through. We want to use our flesh and our own worldly wisdom to address a situation or relationship and solve it. But there are times when God allows defeat or wilderness seasons in our lives as opportunities for growth and development. If we choose not to grow through these times the way He wants us to grow, we will short-circuit His plan. Then we will need to go through a whole other scenario to grow. And the cycle continues.

Whenever you try to jump in and supersede God's plan in your life with your own ways and personal wisdom, you are only delaying the inevitable. You are postponing the strengthening of your spiritual muscles. Look to God during the difficulties of your life and ask Him how He plans to fix or address the situation or strengthen you amid what you are going through. Then, when He shares with you what your part is, obey Him. This way you will reach maturity faster. It is important to wage spiritual warfare from a spiritually mature vantage point, and sometimes it takes challenges and difficulties to get there.

MATTHEW 18:18 *Truly I say to you, whatever you bind on earth shall have been bound in heaven; and whatever you loose on earth shall have been loosed in heaven.*

— 124 —

GOOD DISTRACTIONS

God promises us the power to defeat the enemy in spiritual warfare. But that doesn't mean there's no pain in the process. It's wise to develop a strategy for how to process the pain so that it does not become a hindrance in your fight. For example, in my late fifties, the doctor told me I needed to lose over fifty pounds for health reasons. Walking on a treadmill helped with this.

But the treadmill got boring fast. It also got uncomfortable, and I can honestly say I never once looked forward to it. So for me to be successful at losing the weight, I knew I needed to come up with a strategy for how to process the pain I associated with the treadmill. That's when I decided that while I was huffing and puffing, I would listen to the news. I'm usually a big fan of listening to the news, so it wouldn't take long for me to get caught up in everything going on in the world.

Similarly, when you are going through a painful process as God helps you to overcome the enemy and his attacks in your life, look to Jesus and His Word as a way of orienting your thoughts elsewhere. Ask Him to reveal the good He is doing in your life through this process and fix your thoughts on Christ and His plan for you.

JOHN 15:11 *These things I have spoken to you so that My joy may be in you, and that your joy may be made full.*

—125—

IT'S ALL ABOUT LOVE

In Revelation 2, Jesus criticized the church at Ephesus for leaving its "first love." That criticism may not sound surprising until you discover that they were doing the work of the ministry. They were working for God. It's just that their work itself had become their love and focus, rather than God. Their love for God had started out hot and on fire, but in time, they began to fixate more on the work they did for God rather than on God himself. God wants you to serve Him out of a heart of love. Anything less than that is a waste of your time—and His.

Love is the critical component to a successful spiritual journey. If you lose your first love for God, you cannot expect to maintain any level of success spiritually. It may appear from the outside looking in that you are spiritually successful, but God knows the truth. The church Jesus criticized in Revelation 2 looked successful, but God wanted little to do with them at all. Love is the foundation upon which all you do for God should rest. At the heart of all you think, say, and do must be a true love for God. Satan wants you to downplay the importance of this love for God so that you won't realize how easy it is for him to defeat you when you don't have it. That's why the church in Revelation 2 is so important for us to learn from.

REVELATION 2:4 *But I have this against you, that you have left your first love.*

—126—

DUAL REALITY

One of the things we sometimes forget about Jesus is that He was fully human. But not only was He fully human, He was also fully God. In fact, the baby in the manger made His mother. The baby in the stable made the animals that surrounded Him there. The same Jesus who got thirsty could also walk on water. The same Jesus who got hungry could also turn sardines and crackers into a Moby Dick sandwich. The same Jesus who died on the cross would also rise from the dead. He could do all these things because he was both the first and the last. He was fully God and He was fully human.

One of the things you need to understand as you battle in spiritual warfare is that Jesus also battled the devil when Jesus was vulnerable. Jesus was led out into the desert to be tempted. But the temptations didn't come until He had gone without food for forty days. This made Him more vulnerable. His physical strength was limited due to a lack of food. But even though He lacked physical strength, He still overcame the temptation in the desert. As can you. Jesus wants you to know He understands your difficulties. He understands when you are tempted. You can overcome the enemy if you look to Jesus as your guide.

LUKE 1:37 *For nothing will be impossible with God.*

127

THE COST OF DISCIPLESHIP

Your life as a Christian was designed to be rewarding and fulfilling. But we sometimes get confused into thinking it was designed to be easy. That is not the case. If it has never cost you anything to follow Jesus Christ as Lord, it is because you are not following Jesus Christ as Lord.

Paul told Timothy that all those who live godly in Christ Jesus will suffer persecution (2 Timothy 3:12). Thus, if you've never suffered rejection, defeat, or even loss as a result of your Christian faith, you might want to reexamine how strong your faith really is. Those who follow Jesus fully as His committed kingdom disciples will suffer persecution. Unfortunately, we live in a culture that has condemned suffering in a way that causes us all to want to avoid it. We have a pill for any suffering of any kind, pretty much. We have a distraction for any pain or to make up for any loss. But there is a thing called righteous suffering wherein you are suffering as a result of your commitment to Jesus Christ. This is a suffering for which you should feel honored. You should rejoice in this suffering because you know that God is producing good through the difficulties you are facing. It might not feel good, but God can still produce good through that which hurts.

LUKE 14:28 *For which one of you, when he wants to build a tower, does not first sit down and calculate the cost to see if he has enough to complete it?*

—128—

A TIME FOR INTOLERANCE

Tolerance is one of our modern culture's most valued character traits. But did you know that there's also a time for some godly *intolerance*? For example, when you are sick and you can't tolerate the pain anymore, you go to the doctor. Let's say it's an emergency-level sickness, so you go to the emergency room. You are looking for someone to help you get back to the point where you can tolerate the situation. If you wind up having surgery, the surgeon is not going to tolerate dirt or germs in the operating room or on the surgical instruments. There are times when intolerance is a good thing.

Unfortunately today, *intolerance* has become a negative term. But we are not to tolerate sin in our own lives. God has called us to live according to the standards of His righteousness, and when we tolerate anything less than that, we open ourselves up to soul sickness, disease, and even death. It might be the death of a dream, career, hope, relationship—any number of things—but when we tolerate sin in our life, it opens the door for the devil to wreak havoc. God says that ongoing sin is unacceptable, and it ought not to be tolerated in any way. That's not to say that anyone is perfect and that no one stumbles. But ongoing and unrepented of sin should never be tolerated in a believer's life.

PSALM 145:17 *The Lord is righteous in all His ways and kind in all His deeds.*

—129—

THE NAME OF JESUS CHRIST

Philippians 2:10 tells us that someday, at the name of Jesus, every knee will bow. But today is not that day. You and I are living in what is known as a post-Christian era, when identification with Jesus Christ is increasingly becoming a negative. Those of my generation know what it's like to live in a culture that respected your Christian faith even if they didn't agree with it. There was a respect for the Christian faith and for Jesus Christ. However, children today are growing up in an environment where there is not only a rejection but also a hatred—not of the name God, because that can be vague—but of Jesus Christ.

We are living in a society antagonistic to the claims of Christ, where Jesus' name is regularly taken in vain. So it is all the more important to honor the name of Jesus Christ in all you say and do. There is one main target in Satan's strategy and that is Jesus Christ. He will do whatever he can to defame Jesus. If you want to send Satan a tough punch, lift up and make known the name of Jesus.

As you testify to the power of Jesus Christ in your spheres of influence, you will be delivering blow after blow to the evil one. Continue to make Jesus known in all you do and say, and watch your spiritual victories advance God's kingdom and His agenda all around you.

JOHN 15:1 *I am the true vine, and My Father is the vinedresser.*

—130—

A COSTLY COMPROMISE

Trying too hard not to offend nonbelievers can hinder the work God wants to do in our lives through His Word, which is the "sword of the Spirit" (Ephesians 6:17). With it, He aims to cut away anything in your life that is not glorifying to Him or that has been compromised. Whenever you compromise kingdom values, especially to gain greater standing in society, God will not be mocked.

It might appear that you have gotten away with it because God's wrath is slow at times. And God often allows His wrath to be delivered through the consequences of the sin. But God will have the final say. No compromise will go unnoticed. His Word has made clear what His righteous standard is. You are without excuse if you choose not to read it, study it, memorize it, and apply it. You have access to the sword of the Spirit; the choice to use it is up to you.

Spiritual compromise will also weaken your use of the sword because you will not be handling the Word rightly. You will not be hearing it in a way so as to retain it. Even if you go to church, treat others well, and say that you love God, when you deviate from the standards in His Word, you will compromise your purpose as well as your power to overcome the enemy's attacks.

ROMANS 1:18 *For the wrath of God is revealed from heaven against all ungodliness and unrighteousness of men who suppress the truth in unrighteousness.*

—131—

TRUTH AND LOVE

Some people who back off their beliefs to avoid offending nonbelievers justify it as an act of kindness, not compromise. But according to Scripture, they've missed the point. Now, we are called to love people. But we are not called to love all ideas. That's the distinction.

The issues arise when Christians want to mix them together. They want to make the idea a person's identity, thus stating that if you don't like his or her viewpoint or values, then you don't like him or her. That, then, lays a false guilt trip on you. It's illegitimate guilt. They will even try to pressure you into loving or accepting worldly ideas by saying that if you don't, then you obviously don't love the people who embrace them. But that is also illegitimate guilt. You can love a person while rejecting his or her values or ideas when they go against God's standard.

Loving someone means that you share the truth of God's standard in a kind, honoring way that demonstrates to them their personal worth. Problems arise when people's rejection of an idea or value results in a rejection or dishonoring of the person who holds it. That is wrong. We are called to love. But we are also called to embrace truth. Winning spiritual warfare comes through embracing truth in a spirit of love.

EPHESIANS 4:15 *But speaking the truth in love, we are to grow up in all aspects into Him who is the head, even Christ.*

—132—

KEEP YOURSELF SMALL

No matter who you think you are in the *world's* eyes, all that matters is how you look in *God's* eyes. Many people whom the world lifts up as leaders, as prominent or powerful, are actually small in God's eyes. Many people whom the world ignores or does not even know may appear large in God's eyes. God's view is based on His Word and His kingdom values. That's why it's critical to see yourself from God's viewpoint. No matter what position you hold, how much money you have, or what influence you may wield in this world, only what God thinks about you matters.

God calls each of us to serve Him in humility. That means the greatest in His eyes is the one who is the humblest servant of all. Even if you go on to accomplish great things for God, you must always keep yourself small from your own vantage point. Don't believe all the positive reviews or feedback you may get if it puffs you up. Pride comes before the fall. Humility is a very big deal to God. This is because anything, and everything, you accomplish is a result of His merciful work in your life. Pride is an easy way for Satan to knock believers off track from fighting the good fight well in spiritual battles.

JAMES 4:10 *Humble yourselves in the presence of the Lord, and He will exalt you.*

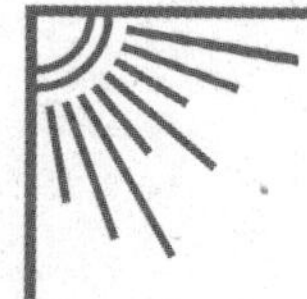

—133—

SELFIE

The Bible makes it clear that God has a problem with idols. He even has a problem with the ones that supposedly remind us of Him. Have you ever had someone take a photo of you that you didn't want anyone to see? Maybe you had an awkward look on your face or the photo wasn't flattering, so you asked the person to delete it.

God doesn't want images, or idols, of himself because anything that we could make to represent God would not come close to His glory. We just don't have the ability to create something to reflect Him well. That's why God only allows one picture of himself for us to worship—and it's a selfie. God's selfie is Jesus Christ. John 1:18 says, "No one has seen God at any time; the only begotten God who is in the bosom of the Father, He has explained Him." To understand and know God is part of spiritual growth and maturity.

Understanding how to fight the good fight in spiritual warfare comes through studying and knowing Jesus Christ. Get to know His character. Study His attributes. Understand what He did during His time on earth, and seek to draw close to Him in relationship. That's the way to access spiritual authority and defeat Satan's attacks in your life.

2 CORINTHIANS 4:6 *For God, who said, "Light shall shine out of darkness," is the One who has shone in our hearts to give the Light of the knowledge of the glory of God in the face of Christ.*

134

HIGHER POINT OF VIEW

It certainly is difficult to wrap our finite brains around an infinite God. And for good reason. For example, when you look at a parade, you see it in parts. You see a band march through. Then you see a float, and maybe another band. But you never see the whole parade at once. Someone in a helicopter, however, can see the entire parade at one time because they are looking down from on high.

Where you are situated determines what you can see. If you look through a keyhole into a room, you can't see the whole room. You can only see what is visible from the keyhole. God is the only one who can see everything all at once. And you have the opportunity to learn from Him, hear from Him, and be guided by Him. Are you still content to trust your own sight when it is limited by your finite mind and body?

The way to defeat Satan and his schemes against you is not easy for you to understand. The exact method to overcome him may be beyond your ability to see. But God knows. That's why drawing close to God and discerning how to hear His voice is imperative. Let Him guide you through this minefield called life. He will tell you where and how to step to get you safely to the other side.

ISAIAH 30:21 *Your ears will hear a word behind you, "This is the way, walk in it," whenever you turn to the right or to the left.*

—135—

ALL FOR HIS GLORY

If you saw a miracle happen every hour of every day, would you start getting used to them? You might come to expect them. They would no longer seem like miracles at all. Keep in mind, miraculous things do take place all around us all the time. For example, eating and drinking are two of the most common and ordinary things we do. Rarely do we even think about the process.

We don't consider the miraculous nature of the human body that can transform a loaded baked potato into nutrition or energy used by our bodies to fuel us. The fact that our bodies are composed of so much water is miraculous in and of itself as well. Maybe that's why we are told in Scripture that whatever we do, we are to glorify God in it—because all that we do is miraculous. First Corinthians 10:31 says, "Whether, then, you eat or drink or whatever you do, do all to the glory of God."

You and I were placed on earth to glorify God. That is our primary purpose. When we move away from that purpose, we move closer to Satan's purpose and thus lose the spiritual battle overall. Always be mindful to consider why you are here. You are here to bring God glory—and He has given you both ordinary and extraordinary ways to do that.

MATTHEW 5:16 *Let your light shine before men in such a way that they may see your good works, and glorify your Father who is in heaven.*

—136—

THE REAL OWNER

You've either heard or said yourself, "My house, my rules." But what would change if you suddenly realized it wasn't your house? Psalm 135:6 says, "Whatever the LORD pleases, He does, in heaven and in earth, in the seas and in all deeps." Psalm 24:1 says, "The earth is the LORD's, and all it contains, the world, and those who dwell in it." This earth is God's house. He created it. He is the absolute ruler, owner, controller, sustainer, and provider of all things. It's His house. And His rules.

What would you think if someone came to your house and started telling you how to decorate it without your permission? They aren't paying the mortgage so what say should they have? Or what if someone came to your house uninvited and made themselves something to eat? You might call the police. You have a right to your rules in your home.

We live in God's house, and to fight the good fight, we must fight according to His rules. One of His preeminent rules is that we bring Him glory in all that we think, say, and do. When we fail to do that, we cannot expect to have His backing, and we cannot bank on His provision. God supplies for His plans, and His plan is that we glorify Him in all we choose to do.

ISAIAH 43:7 *Everyone who is called by My name, and whom I have created for My glory, whom I have formed, even whom I have made.*

—137—

GOD'S SOVEREIGN BOUNDARIES

It's popular these days to rebel against authority and challenge any boundaries we might find in our way. But life needs rules and boundaries. Authority is important for things to run smoothly. When God set up the nation of Israel in Old Testament days, He gave them many rules and regulations that were important for maintaining health and order.

We often forget that rules are for our own good when given by a loving authority. On the football field, you have sovereign, nonnegotiable lines, such as sidelines, goal lines, hash lines, and more. Without these lines, there would be no game. It is because of the rules and regulations that football is a sport to enjoy.

God's righteous standards are His boundary lines for life. Living within those lines ushers in His favor. It provides us with the opportunity to live out our purpose as well as to defeat the enemy. Sure, there are times when we foul, or cross the line. That is when we must look to Jesus for forgiveness and resume the game. Never let Satan convince you that you have fouled out of this game of life. Jesus' death on the cross paid the ultimate price so that you and I could serve the Lord our entire lives and commit our paths to Him upon returning and repenting—choosing to stay within His sovereign righteous lines.

ROMANS 12:1 *Therefore I urge you, brethren, by the mercies of God, to present your bodies a living and holy sacrifice, acceptable to God, which is your spiritual service of worship.*

—138—

AWED BY GOD

How would you react if you met God face-to-face? A woman went to an ice cream shop to get a cone. Standing behind her was her favorite actor. As she was paying for her ice cream, she caught a glimpse of him. His presence made her speechless. In fact, she couldn't even continue to pay. She just left her ice-cream cone in the hand of the attendant as she turned around and walked out of the store.

Once she was outside, a man came up to her carrying the ice-cream cone. It was her favorite actor. "You forgot your cone," he said. Her mind was so consumed by his presence that she had lost her appetite. She didn't even want her ice cream anymore.

Far too often we take God for granted and yet He exists all around us. His presence is near to us. We just cannot see Him. But could we see Him, we would be overwhelmed knowing that we are standing in the presence of God the Creator. Pray and ask the Holy Spirit to open your spiritual eyes to see God's presence near you. He *is* near. Once you realize how near He truly is, sin's pull will no longer be so strong. You might even lose your appetite for what Satan uses to tempt you.

ISAIAH 6:3 *And one called out to another and said, "Holy, Holy, Holy, is the LORD of hosts, the whole earth is full of His glory."*

Just as light always
drives out darkness,
God will always
drive out Satan.

139

WHERE CAN YOU STEP?

When God's glory fills a place, the place is so full there is no room for anything else. If you want to drive out Satan's influence in your life, all you need to do is invite in God's glory. Just as light always drives out darkness, God will always drive out Satan. When God's presence is made manifest in your heart and mind, Satan will have no room to launch his attacks on you. Spend time meditating on God's Word and filling yourself with His truth. Daily time in His Word is one way to fill your thoughts with His presence. Another way is through prayer.

God's glory filled His whole throne room, Isaiah told us in the book named after Him. Wherever God is, He takes up all the space. Just like a woman who walks down the aisle on her wedding day with a long train flowing from her dress and filling the aisle, the train of God's robe fills the entire place where we are to walk. We are to follow Him and allow His presence to guide and consume us. This will have a profound impact on your spiritual battles. You will find Satan's attacks less and less successful against you because he cannot remain in the presence of the Lord when His glory fills the place. There's simply no room for him.

ISAIAH 6:4 *And the foundations of the thresholds trembled at the voice of him who called out, while the temple was filling with smoke.*

—140—

WHY EVIL EXISTS

If God made everything, did He also make evil? It's a question people have been asking for centuries. God doesn't create evil. But He did create choice. God gave us free will, allowing us to choose evil. Since sin entered the world through Adam, we have had an open door for evil to proliferate. In fact, it got so bad during Noah's time that God sent a flood to wipe the people from the face of the earth and start again through Noah's lineage.

Free will allows you and me freedom and liberty. But freedom is never free. It comes with a cost: We can choose evil. Thus, Satan is constantly trying to get us to choose poorly. The more evil Satan can stir up in our hearts and minds, the less likely we are to serve and glorify God.

Although evil exists, God works to turn what is meant for evil into good. We see this in the powerful story of Joseph. We read in Genesis 50:20, "As for you, you meant evil against me, but God meant it for good in order to bring about this present result, to preserve many people alive." Even though evil exists, and you may have failed in ways you regret, when you turn to God and seek His face and glory above all, He can turn what was meant for evil into something for good.

GENESIS 50:20 *As for you, you meant evil against me, but God meant it for good in order to bring about this present result, to preserve many people alive.*

—141—

GOING FOR THE BREAD

Jesus turning a small amount of food into enough to feed thousands is recorded more than any other miracle in the Gospels. It happened two years into Jesus' ministry, and His popularity was going through the roof. John 6 records that the miracle happened during the Passover, the celebration of Israel's deliverance from Egypt when the death angel passed over every house covered by the blood as recorded in Exodus 11:1–12:36. John wanted his readers to make the connection between Israel under Egypt's oppression and Israel under Rome's oppression.

The Old Testament prophesied that when Messiah came, He would deliver His people and bring in a new kingdom. Thus, by this time many Jews thought that's what Jesus would do. The problem was that the people wanted the miracles and bread Jesus was offering, but they didn't want the message He was preaching.

They were saying, "Jesus is our man to heal us, feed us, and lead us out of Roman bondage." The crowds grew because the people wanted to see what Jesus would do next. But looking to Jesus just for bread and miracles isn't a relationship. You might get the bread, but you won't gain access to the spiritual authority you need to defeat the enemy's schemes.

EXODUS 12:23 *For the LORD will pass through to smite the Egyptians; and when He sees the blood on the lintel and on the two doorposts, the LORD will pass over the door and will not allow the destroyer to come in to your houses to smite you.*

—142—

OUR CARING SHEPHERD

Jesus knows where you are and what you're going through. What's more: He cares. When the huge crowd gathered around Him just before He fed them with the miraculous bread, Jesus looked out and saw broken people with broken lives. They had brought their sick and their lame. Jesus felt compassion for them. That tells us that Jesus Christ is more than just a Person of power. He is One who cares.

Jesus feels your pain. The beauty of the incarnation is that when God became man, He could feel what we feel. How many times have you been deceived into going to the wrong places, doing the wrong things, thinking the wrong thoughts, or hanging out with the wrong people? Satan strives for these things regularly. But you are only deceived when you forget to look to Jesus and trust His heart.

Jesus understands your difficulties and temptations. He was fully God and fully human. That's why Jesus is the only One who can be the mediator between God and us. But Jesus can do much more than sympathize with you. His power can overrule your circumstances. His compassion can deal with your situation. He healed the sick that day (Matthew 14:14), but He fed them too. I don't know what situation you might be facing today as you wage spiritual warfare, but when you bring Jesus Christ into the equation, you have someone who can surmount the insurmountable.

MATTHEW 14:14 *When He went ashore, He saw a large crowd, and felt compassion for them and healed their sick.*

—143—

THIS IS A TEST

The miracle of turning the food into enough bread to feed thousands happened at an interesting time in the disciples' lives. In Mark 6:31 we read that the disciples were tired. They wanted to dismiss the crowd and send them home. But Jesus instructed them to take care of the crowd's growing hunger and asked how they planned to do it. John 6:6 says, "This He was saying to test him, for He Himself knew what He was intending to do."

Philip had been with Jesus around two years by then. He had seen Him change water into wine. He had seen Jesus heal people. But unfortunately for Philip, he relied on his own wisdom and let Jesus know they simply didn't have enough money to feed everyone. Apparently, Philip forgot who he was talking to.

When Jesus asks you a question, you should know He already has the answer. Jesus doesn't really need your help—He's just trying to see if you understand the way He functions. Sometimes He will also put you in a test to see if your faith in Him has grown or if you are still trying to figure things out on your own. Pass the test and you will unleash the ability to witness Jesus perform miracles in your own struggles and challenges.

JOHN 6:5 *Therefore Jesus, lifting up His eyes and seeing that a large crowd was coming to Him, said to Philip, "Where are we to buy bread, so that these may eat?"*

—144—

ASK AND BELIEVE

We can tell from Philip's answer to Jesus about not having enough money to feed the thousands of people that he didn't have much hope of anything being done about the circumstance they were facing. We know this because all he could see was how little they had. But there was another disciple on the scene, Peter's brother Andrew.

Philip said, "Forget it." Andrew said, "I've been scouring around, and I found a boy with his lunch." Barley loaves were little pancakes. They were poor people's food. It would be like us having sardines and crackers for dinner. While Philip saw no way the people could be fed, at least Andrew saw some hope. Not much, to be sure. He still had limited vision. But what can or can't be done is never the question when Jesus is on the scene. The issue is the will of God, not the size of the problem.

Regardless of what you're facing, the question is always, What is the will of God? He can always afford whatever He chooses to do. There is never a lack of resources with God. When you go up against the enemy and all his strategies to defeat you, never allow scarcity to be a stumbling block. You are connected to the Creator of the universe through the Lord Jesus Christ. He has more than enough to meet any need you have. Just ask and believe.

MATTHEW 7:7 *Ask, and it will be given to you; seek, and you will find; knock, and it will be opened to you.*

—145—

IN EVERYTHING GIVE THANKS

There is a wonderful contrast between the way Jesus responded to the situation with the crowd needing to be fed and the way His disciples responded. His disciples complained, wanted to send everyone away, and lost hope. I imagine we would have complained too. But Jesus gave thanks.

I'll bet when Jesus said, "Let us give thanks," Philip and Andrew were looking at each other thinking, *Give thanks for what?* But Jesus was thankful for what He had. Some of us might have started our prayer with, "How come I only have crackers and sardines? Lord, You promised to meet all my needs, and I need more than this."

One of the tragedies today is that we don't have enough Christians who know how to give thanks for what they have. Jesus gave thanks for two reasons: He had something, and He was anticipating more. Did Jesus need more than five loaves and two fish to feed five thousand men, plus women and children? Of course. But He knew what Paul later told us in Philippians 4:6, "Be anxious for nothing, but in everything by prayer and supplication with thanksgiving let your requests be made known to God." Don't come to God without saying thanks first.

And don't approach spiritual warfare without thanking God. Remember, you are not fighting *for* victory; you are fighting *from* victory. In Jesus, you have already won. Thank Him for that victory every day.

EPHESIANS 5:20 *Always giving thanks for all things in the name of our Lord Jesus Christ to God, even the Father.*

—146—

BE THANKFUL FOR ACCESS

When you kneel before our all-powerful God, the equation changes. When you give thanks to God for not enough, trusting He can make it more than enough, you have already won. There is a new agenda you have just brought to the table—the glory of God.

If God's people really got hold of this, we would stop clutching our five barley loaves and two fish, afraid we won't have anything left. We would be more like the young boy with the small lunch in the story, saying to the Lord, "Here is what I have. Take it, because I know that if I give it to You, something good will be done with it."

The truth is that for many of us, circumstances are working out pretty well. We're doing better than we've ever done financially. The family is healthy and intact. If that's true, don't forget God, or you'll be poorer than when you had less. If you don't bring God into the equation, it doesn't matter what you have. It will never be enough, because if you forget God, you're putting your wealth into a bag full of holes (Haggai 1:6). But when you bring what you have to God, He can do amazing things with it. Thank Him for making access to the Father possible, so you will never have to go without, or lose what you have—when you trust Him.

1 CHRONICLES 16:8 *Oh give thanks to the LORD, call upon His name; make known His deeds among the peoples.*

—147—

A REASON TO REJOICE

If you are not in the middle of a challenging situation right now, just hang around a bit. None of us can dodge challenging situations.

Trials are not designed to sink your boat, but rather to help you improve your navigation skills. We can rejoice when we undergo trials, because we know God is doing something special in our lives. "Consider it all joy, my brethren, when you encounter various trials, knowing that the testing of your faith produces endurance. And let endurance have its perfect result, so that you may be perfect and complete, lacking in nothing" (James 1:2–4).

Sometimes God sends a trial to teach you a specific lesson. At other times, it comes simply because you live in a sin-cursed world, and the consequences of sin rub off on you, like when you're the victim of a crime or accident. Sometimes trials are the result of your sin. You yield to a temptation that leads to a set of circumstances that are tough to deal with. And don't forget that the enemy can attack you with trials, hoping for your spiritual defeat.

The good news is, you're not out there alone, because no matter what the source of your trial is, God has the situation well in hand. He can work out His purposes even in a trial you bring on yourself. But He will only do that if you humble yourself before Him and rejoice for the good work He is bringing about.

PHILIPPIANS 4:4 *Rejoice in the Lord always; again I will say, rejoice!*

—148—

TRUST JESUS IN THE STORM

Matthew 8:18–27 is a classic story of a trial by storm. Matthew says that the disciples followed Jesus into the boat, which means that this trip was Jesus' idea, not theirs. The disciples wanted to stay where they were because Jesus had just miraculously fed five thousand men. They were just like the crowd who wanted to make Jesus their welfare king. But Jesus wanted no part of it.

What the disciples wanted and what they needed were two different things. They wanted royalty, but what they got was a rowboat in a storm. Because that's what Jesus wanted them to have, and was what they needed.

The disciples were soon battered by the waves and wind. The harder they rowed, the harder the wind pushed in the other direction. Mark depicts them "straining at the oars" (Mark 6:48). Are you in a storm today? For a Christian, there is no such thing as random, pointless trials. If Jesus sent you into the storm, His authority is reigning over it. God can hit a bull's-eye even with a crooked stick. He can take a trial caused by your sin and failure and still make something good come out of it, but you have to trust Him in the storm. That's easier said than done, but it's the only way through.

MARK 6:48 *Seeing them straining at the oars, for the wind was against them, at about the fourth watch of the night He came to them, walking on the sea; and He intended to pass by them.*

—149—

TRADE YOUR FEAR FOR FAITH

When the disciples were on the boat in the middle of a storm, Jesus came walking to them on the water as recorded in Matthew 14:22–33. One of the most important points to take from this story is that Jesus knows right where you are. Even though it may be dark, the wind may be howling, and you might only be able to see a foot in front of you, Jesus can see you. You are not alone. Jesus can find you even in the dark. There's no darkness to Him.

Realize not only that Jesus will arrive on time during your difficulties or battles in spiritual warfare, but also that what you see isn't all there is to be seen. What the disciples thought was a serious problem in the storm—a ghost coming out to them—turned out to be their salvation in the person of Jesus. The very thing that might look like the worst problem for you may be the thing the Savior uses to deliver you.

What you see as a source of fear may be God's way of saying, "Take courage; I'm here." Trials have a way of clouding your vision so that you might not really be seeing what you think you're seeing. That's why you must always look for Christ and trade your fear for faith.

HEBREWS 12:2 *Fixing our eyes on Jesus, the author and perfecter of faith, who for the joy set before Him endured the cross, despising the shame, and has sat down at the right hand of the throne of God.*

— 150 —

THE FLOW OF JESUS

When airlines first started transatlantic flights to Europe, they noticed that sometimes the plane would arrive an hour or so ahead of schedule without the wear and tear on the engine expected for flights of that length. The engineers could not understand it, because they didn't know as much about the weather as we do today.

So as they began trying to figure out how this could happen, they discovered a weather phenomenon known today as the jet stream. When an airplane gets into the jet stream, it is propelled by the wind so that even though it is being flown at the same air speed as a plane not in the jet stream, it is really going faster, because it is carried along by the jet stream winds.

Thus, rather than fighting the air currents, a plane in the jet stream is being carried on the air. Your trials or spiritual battles may have you in turbulence right now. You may feel as if you're flying in the face of a strong wind, just like the disciples who rowed against a strong wind in Matthew 14. But what you need to do is catch the Jesus stream. When you catch the flow of the Jesus stream, He will carry you where you need to go. He will get you there ahead of schedule, and you won't experience all the wear and tear you would if you tried to go it alone.

MATTHEW 14:33 *And those who were in the boat worshiped Him, saying, "You are certainly God's Son!"*

—151—

YOU ARE A KNOWN TARGET

Spiritual warfare started when the devil challenged the authority of God in heaven and led his coup d'etat. Satan's influence must have been enormous because a third of the angels followed him. These fallen angels came to be known as demons or unclean spirits. They are the devil's army, his foot soldiers. They are the denizens of hell, a place created to be the eternal prison for Satan and his angels.

Satan has emulated heaven in creating an organizational structure. He crafted a demonic government whose job it is to carry out hell's agenda in thwarting God's kingdom agenda. Our battle is against this government of demons.

The words Paul uses in Ephesians 6:12 to describe hell's hierarchy are governmental terms lifted right out of the ruling Roman regime. *Rulers* refers to those demonic princes who guide the affairs of the satanic realm. *Powers* execute Satan's program. Under them are the *forces* of darkness, the workhorses, the lieutenants and sergeants who make sure those programs are properly implemented. Finally, there are the wicked spirits who take the marching orders to the field of battle.

When you became a Christian, you became a target. You became a named and known enemy of Satan. You are in spiritual warfare whether you realize it, or want to be in it, or not.

REVELATION 12:9 *And the great dragon was thrown down, the serpent of old who is called the devil and Satan, who deceives the whole world; he was thrown down to the earth, and his angels were thrown down with him.*

—152—

MAKING DEMONS FLEE

In Mark 5, we have a premier case of demon activity. We're introduced to a madman with an "unclean spirit" who lived in the realm of death. He came out of the tombs. If he lived today, he might binge-watch horror shows.

We learn from verse 4 that he possessed unusual strength. He was also suicidal and ran around without clothes, which is a stark picture of the degradation demons try to heap on human beings.

The man was in torment because of the demons, but the demons were in torment when Jesus showed up. Why? Because Jesus was speaking. There is a spiritual war going on, and I've never heard of a war where there wasn't conflict. The demons begged Jesus not to cast them out because demons only fulfill their reason for living when they are tormenting others. They exist to perpetuate and extend the agenda of hell. But when Jesus said go, they had to go. The power of Christ over demons is the power in which you can stand against the forces of hell.

JOHN 8:44 *You are of your father the devil, and you want to do the desires of your father. He was a murderer from the beginning, and does not stand in the truth because there is no truth in him. Whenever he speaks a lie, he speaks from his own nature, for he is a liar and the father of lies.*

—153—

THE ONLY ONE

In the conclusion of the story of the demon-possessed man, when Jesus ordered the demons out of him, they wanted to enter pigs. Jesus granted them permission to teach an object lesson. This man was written off as insane, and Jesus wanted to show that he wasn't insane—he was under demonic influence. When the demons entered the pigs, they immediately committed suicide.

You can be grazing one minute, and the next minute go downhill so fast that your life isn't worth a dime. That's what demons can do. No matter what counsel you get for your problems, unless you get help from Jesus Christ, you are going to plunge downhill and be drowned in the circumstances of life. You say, "Tony, I'm not Jesus. Jesus could speak, and the demons would leave. How do I have power over demons today?" Jesus told His disciples in Luke 10:20 not to get excited because they had authority over demons, but to get excited because their names were written in the Lamb's Book of Life in heaven. Jesus was saying, "Get excited about what your salvation has done for you."

You don't need to go look for an exorcist. You need to understand who you are in Christ. In Christ you have authority. In Christ you are equipped for spiritual warfare.

LUKE 10:21 *At that very time He rejoiced greatly in the Holy Spirit, and said, "I praise You, O Father, Lord of heaven and earth, that You have hidden these things from the wise and intelligent and have revealed them to infants.*

— 154 —

THE THREE R'S

Satan and his demons are real. They are dangerous and clever. But they are also beaten enemies in the power of Christ. Let me give you three R's for dealing with demonic attacks. First, *recall* what Christ has done for you in relationship to the demonic realm. Read Colossians 2:14–15 and 1 Peter 3:22. We are not just talking about what Jesus did on earth, but what is happening now while He is seated at the right hand of God. The demons are subject to Him.

Second, *resist* the devil. James 4:7 says, "Submit therefore to God. Resist the devil and he will flee from you." This is not just the power of positive thinking. Resisting Satan includes submitting to God. To submit to God means not compromising with the devil's agenda. Resist Satan by putting on the full armor of God.

Finally, *rely* on God to do in and through you what you could never do yourself. If you could live the Christian life on your own, God would not have to indwell you by the Holy Spirit. You need a power bigger than yourself, someone experienced in this kind of warfare. The Holy Spirit is a seasoned general who's been fighting demons for a long time. He knows how, when, and where they move. When you are filled with the Spirit and submitted to God, you are well armed.

LUKE 10:19 *Behold, I have given you authority to tread on serpents and scorpions, and over all the power of the enemy, and nothing will injure you.*

—155—

OPERATION BREADBASKET

You remember what happened with the first Adam when Satan tempted him in the garden of Eden. Satan came onto God's territory, got Adam to sin, and as a result, Adam was kicked out of a garden into a wilderness. But the last Adam (Jesus) paid Satan a return visit on his territory. Jesus went into the wilderness to defeat Satan and get back for us what was lost by the failure of our forefather.

By His victory, Jesus reclaimed us from the wilderness so He could one day bring us to the paradise of God, which is heaven. God does not tempt anyone (James 1:13). But He does test us. What's the difference? Testing is designed to validate our victory in Christ. But tempting by the devil is designed to defeat us spiritually.

To clarify, Jesus came under Satan's temptation in the wilderness, as described in Matthew 4. Jesus had fasted for forty days and nights in preparation for the spiritual battle. His first temptation was what I'll call "Operation Breadbasket." The devil had been watching Jesus fast. He knew Jesus was hungry. Satan tried to get Jesus to question God's provision, basically saying, "God hasn't given You what You need." But Jesus responded with the Word of God, "It is written." If Jesus answered temptation with the Word, how much more do we need to use the Word against our enemy?

JAMES 1:17 *Every good thing given and every perfect gift is from above, coming down from the Father of lights, with whom there is no variation or shifting shadow.*

156

GO AHEAD AND JUMP

The devil knows the Bible. During Jesus' temptation in the wilderness, he even tried out Jesus' own words on Him: "It is written" (Matthew 4:6). Why did Satan do this? He was saying to Jesus, "I can't get You to act independently of God, so let me work through Your religion." Satan did something similar to Eve in the garden. And he got Eve to question God's Word.

Satan summed up to Jesus, "Since you don't want to act independently of God, let's put it all on God." He took Jesus to the pinnacle of the temple, about four hundred feet up, and quoted Scripture to Him about how God would have the angels catch Jesus if He jumped. This, by the way, would show His messiahship to Israel, as He miraculously floated down to earth. Thus, the second temptation was to question the plan of God.

Satan is cunning and clever. He offered to help Jesus fulfill God's plan for His life. After all, He was the Messiah, wasn't He? What would be wrong with proving it? Let me tell you something: God does not need Satan's help to get you where He wants you to go. How did Jesus respond? He used God's Word again. If you're going to defeat Satan, imitate Jesus. Know God's Word so well that no one can fool you into trying to achieve God's will by taking shortcuts.

1 THESSALONIANS 5:6 *So then let us not sleep as others do, but let us be alert and sober.*

—157—

TIME TO TAKE A BOW

By the time we get to temptation number three in the wilderness in this contest between Jesus and Satan, the enemy has cut right to the bottom line. By offering Jesus the kingdoms of the world in return for His worship, Satan has taken off his covering and is standing there with horns, a pitchfork, and a red jumpsuit, saying, "Jesus, let me tell You what I'm getting at. Bow! Kneel before me now."

That's what Satan wants from you too. He might not come out and say so at first. He didn't with Jesus. But Satan really is saying, "Worship me." This final temptation, described in Matthew 4:8–9, is the most blatant. No quoting of Scripture, just a straight-up offer of power and wealth if Jesus would acknowledge Satan as His master.

That's what Satan is after in your life and mine. He wants us to make him God. That is what he has always wanted, to exalt his throne above the throne of God. And some of us have bowed. We have bowed at the altar of materialism. Our passion for stuff has driven us from God. When we were poor, we worshiped and made time for God. Now that we have stuff, we don't. Or we have bowed at the altar of pleasure, self, sports, or other things. Whatever it is, it is never worth it to kneel before Satan. You will regret it.

DEUTERONOMY 6:13 *You shall fear only the LORD your God; and you shall worship Him and swear by His name.*

—158—

WORSHIP AND SERVE

Did you know you have no obligation at all to the devil? When Jesus got tired of the mess with Satan in the wilderness, He told Satan to get lost. We owe the devil nothing. You do not owe him your time, worship, or service. Still, too many of us worship God on Sunday, then serve Satan all week.

Based on Jesus' temptation, I believe that if you resist the devil three times about any one temptation, he must leave you at that time when you use the Word. You say, "Well, he's not fleeing from me. He's all over me!" Maybe you are not using the Word. The devil is not impressed by what you know or think. He only leaves when the Word of God comes into play.

Jesus hit Satan three times with God's Word, and Satan left. Then angels showed up. Sometimes God leaves you with only His Word to see if you know how to use it. Once you use it, God can send angels to minister to you, just as He did for Jesus. But that wasn't until the battle was over. Don't wait for help to arrive in your spiritual battle. Fight the good fight now. But remember, you can't overcome or resist the devil on your own. But you can beat him in Christ's authority using the Word of God.

REVELATION 12:11 *And they overcame him because of the blood of the Lamb and because of the word of their testimony, and they did not love their life even when faced with death.*

—159—

THE GOOD FIGHT

Suppose you were at home one night when a gigantic intruder broke into your house and took over. He held you hostage in your house. He was strong and scary. Nothing you did would intimidate him or make him leave. Then you remembered you just had to call 911. If you could reach a phone when the intruder wasn't looking and dial 911, then help would come.

Once you were able to do that, the police arrived at your door to help. This is because they got a distress call from you. Similarly, Satan is an intruder in your life. He is an intruder in your spiritual home. He has come to destroy and take over your life, holding you hostage to sin. But God has an emergency line too. That emergency number is His Word. When you use His Word, the firepower from heaven comes down to remove the intruder from your spiritual home. When you call out to God based on His Word, heaven will provide all you need to get the intruder out of your home.

Fighting the good fight involves knowing which punches to pull and which punches to throw. Pull your own punches because they won't land well on the enemy. But throw the punches that come from God's Word. That is what will defeat the enemy in spiritual warfare.

1 Timothy 6:12 *Fight the good fight of faith; take hold of the eternal life to which you were called, and you made the good confession in the presence of many witnesses.*

— 160 —

BOUNCING BACK

In basketball, rebounding is such a valuable skill because there are so many missed shots. That's also true in life. In fact, if you haven't missed any shots yet, just keep playing. After a missed shot, the thing to do is get that rebound and get back in the game.

There are a number of examples of this in the Bible, including Joseph, David, Jonah, and Peter. Maybe you can identify with them and learn how to keep fighting the good fight even after you have messed up. God can transform your circumstances—or your relationship to your circumstances—if you allow His sovereignty to work in your life.

God wants to take the mess of your life—the sins you've repented of, the broken relationships, and broken circumstances—and transform it into something good. While He's doing that, don't try to ignore the past or pretend it never happened. Ask God to "make up to you," in His time and in His way, whatever it is you have lost (Joel 2:25). Make a commitment to God to keep going and keep trying. One of Satan's primary strategies is to get each of us to give up. He will use shame, blame, or regret to do this. Never let a missed shot, or a past sin, keep you from living wholeheartedly for God right now.

JOEL 2:25 *Then I will make up to you for the years that the swarming locust has eaten, the creeping locust, the stripping locust and the gnawing locust, My great army which I sent among you.*

161

A ROUGH START

There aren't many of us who don't get broken sometime, somehow. One area where all of us have experienced this is in broken relationships. Because we are all sinners, when we start relating to one another, things get broken. It might go back to childhood, when you were rejected by your father or mother. You may have a history of abuse, betrayal, and divorce. Or you may have friends or loved ones you don't talk to anymore. Broken relationships come in all shapes, sizes, and degrees. But God is aware of any broken relationship you may be suffering from today, and He has a word of hope and healing for you.

The last fourteen chapters of Genesis record Joseph's remarkable life and give insight into fortifying our relationships so Satan can't use them to trip us up again. After all, Joseph didn't come from an ideal family, to say the least. He was the eleventh son of Jacob, the master deceiver. By this time Jacob had gotten his spiritual act together, but his ten older sons took after dad. They once deceived and killed an entire city of men because one of the men had raped their sister (see Genesis 34, especially v. 13). Joseph had a lot going against him, yet the Bible presents him to us as a man of greatness and dignity. He is a reminder that with God's help, you can rise above your family history.

GENESIS 34:13 *But Jacob's sons answered Shechem and his father Hamor with deceit, because he had defiled Dinah their sister.*

—162—

GOD IS FOR YOU

Perhaps you have been rejected at some point in life. Maybe you discovered that the people you thought loved you didn't really love you at all. That sounds a lot like Joseph's story. He was sold like an animal by his own brothers. Can you imagine the feeling of rejection? After that, Joseph found himself in a hostile land. But Genesis 39:2 says, "The Lord was with Joseph, so he became a successful man." Joseph may have come from a rough home and had a rough start, but God was with Joseph. Though he was sold into slavery, God managed to make Joseph into a successful man in the land.

Even when the people you love don't want you, if you stay with the Lord, you can still get somewhere. Joseph was rejected by his loved ones, but he was accepted by the Lord. Regardless of what happened to you yesterday, if you remain faithful to the Lord today, He can control your tomorrow. Don't fall for Satan's lie. He often uses broken relationships to convince people they cannot have a successful future or a thriving spiritual life. The fact is that some relationships are not going to be fixed. You may never get your parents to accept you. You may never be able to completely heal some relationships. But the Lord can take you where you are and still make you a success.

GENESIS 39:3 *Now his master saw that the Lord was with him and how the Lord caused all that he did to prosper in his hand.*

—163—

FALSELY ACCUSED

Have you ever wondered why Joseph turned out much better than his older brothers? I have an idea. Joseph's father, Jacob, was a spiritual mess for a long time. But when he got older, he wrestled with God and received His blessing (Genesis 32:22–29). Jacob made a decision for God that Joseph was able to benefit from because he was still at home.

If you get right with God, He can help you get right with your kids, especially those still at home. Jacob could not undo the past, but he could walk with God in the present and see God bless his life in spite of his past. He raised Joseph to be committed to a holy life. This was evident when, as a slave, Joseph resisted the sexual advances of his master's wife. He saw that his situation could only be explained by the hand of God, and he refused Potiphar's wife.

Potiphar's wife, who felt scorned, made it her mission to ruin Joseph's life. She falsely accused him of rape, sending Joseph to jail. But as we saw earlier in Joseph's life, God was with him. Even in jail, Joseph was not alone, and God prospered Joseph to make him successful and to find favor even in prison. God can take other people's hatred or scorn of you and prosper you in the midst of it, if you will trust Him in the process.

GENESIS 32:30 *So Jacob named the place Peniel, for he said, "I have seen God face to face, yet my life has been preserved."*

—164—

FROM THE PRISON TO THE PALACE

You might not always understand why God has you in a certain place, but if you are committed to Him and serving His purposes, He can make even bad places produce a good result. Take Joseph in jail, for example. At this point in his life, there was no better place for Joseph to be than in jail because he was right where God wanted him to be.

By now the spiritual warfare principle ought to be obvious: Even when you walk with God, human relationships can still get broken, but if you focus on God, Satan cannot use them to get you offtrack. Sometimes God must take you to the bottom in order to take you to the top. The hard part is remembering when you hit bottom that it's not the end of the trip. Lasting hope for spiritually rebounding and making it through spiritual warfare well is found in commitment to Christ. In Genesis 40, you will read that Joseph wound up helping one of Pharaoh's officials in jail, but the man forgot about Joseph when he got out. Joseph remained in jail two more years. But he was not alone. God was with him, and Joseph honored God in his actions. As a result, he eventually got out and was promoted into a powerful position. Never let your circumstances cause you to lose hope. God can create miracles out of any and every situation, if you will trust Him.

GENESIS 40:23 *Yet the chief cupbearer did not remember Joseph, but forgot him.*

—165—

GOOD OUT OF BAD

Once Joseph got out of prison, he was promoted to the second most powerful position in the land. His brothers were in need. Their people were starving, so they had come to Egypt for help. Joseph hadn't forgotten what they had done to him. But he also knew that God had used what they had done to him for good. It was because of what they had done with ill intent that he was now in a position of power.

God can do the same for you. Maybe someone who hurt you took part of your life away, but God can give it back to you. You don't have an excuse for not doing anything for God right now. Anyone who tells you, "Just forget it," is not living in the real world. It happened, and you might always remember it. But God can do something good with it, or despite it, if you will commit your ways to Him.

Later in Joseph's story we read that God gave Joseph his own family. One reason old relationships may be destroying you is that you haven't replaced them with new relationships. You are hanging out with the wrong reminders. God helped Joseph to forget the pain of what happened. He still had the memory, but it no longer hurt like it once did. You might not be able to forget your past. But it doesn't have to control your tomorrow.

GENESIS 50:22 *Now Joseph stayed in Egypt, he and his father's household, and Joseph lived one hundred and ten years.*

— 166 —

DO NOT BE QUICK TO CUT OFF AN EAR

Peter is one of the most colorful characters in the Bible. Given Peter's nature, it's not surprising that he missed some shots and had some spiritual rebounding to do. Peter was a key figure in all the events of Jesus' last days on earth. In Matthew 26:33 we read, "But Peter said to Him, 'Even though all may fall away because of You, I will never fall away.'" Peter made bold statements. And it's possible he even believed them. But Jesus knew better.

A lot of us are like Peter. We have good intentions. We vow great spiritual vows. We publicly declare what we will do, only to find our lives collapse around us one day. Almost any believer can find something to identify with in the life of Peter.

In John 18 we find the story of Jesus and the disciples in the garden. When soldiers came to arrest Jesus, Peter whacked off the ear of a man named Malchus. On a human level, we might applaud Peter. We might say, "Good for him!" But Jesus rebuked Peter, who had missed the point. We need to make sure we are not analyzing events from a worldly point of view, but rather from a spiritual, kingdom point of view. Jumping in with the wrong solution rather than looking to God for His leading will only lead to destruction.

JOHN 18:11 *So Jesus said to Peter, "Put the sword into the sheath; the cup which the Father has given Me, shall I not drink it?"*

—167—

DISASTER IN THE GARDEN

In the garden of Gethsemane, the disciple Peter might have fought a good fight, but he fought the wrong fight. If you take out your own sword (meaning human methodology) when God wants to give you His cup of suffering (His divine will), you will not have God's backing. When you adopt man's way rather than God's way, you interfere with the plan of God for your life and leave yourself open to even greater spiritual attack.

Peter used man's way to defend Jesus. Not only that, but we find out from Matthew 26:36–46 that when he was supposed to be praying earlier, he was sleeping. And Peter was also being disobedient here, because when Jesus told the soldiers to let the disciples "go their way" (John 18:8), I believe He was essentially telling Peter and the others, "Leave here and go back home. You don't need to be part of this." In fact, John adds in verse 9 that Jesus said what He did to fulfill His own prophecy that none of His disciples would be lost. In other words, Jesus was acting to save Peter's life by trying to get him out of there. Let's summarize: Peter was prayerless, worldly, and disobedient. That's a lethal combination. When you have a weak prayer life, when you're thinking like the secular world thinks rather than like God thinks, and when you're not doing what God tells you to do, you're a sitting duck for the forces of hell.

JOHN 18:27 *Peter then denied it again, and immediately a rooster crowed.*

168

REMAIN VIGILANT

In the early hours after the arrest of Jesus, what was left of Peter's spiritual life came unglued. A servant girl said, "You look a lot like one of those guys who were hanging out with Jesus." Peter answered, "Me? No, you've got me mixed up with someone else."

They were all standing around the fire getting warm when denial number two occurred. Finally, Peter was challenged by a servant who was a relative of Malchus, the man whose ear Peter had cut off. This guy was more sure of Peter's identity, so Peter had to make his point very clear. Mark 14:71 says he denied Christ with a curse. Peter wasn't just swearing like a sailor here. He swore an oath known as a *self-maledictory* oath, which means you take an oath against yourself. You swear that if you are lying, judgment will be brought on you. This is no small thing, because swearing a self-maledictory oath could cost you your life.

Most of us would say, "That's terrible. He denied Christ. I would never do that." But have we ever denied Christ before others by the way we live? If we confessed Christ, would the people we know be shocked because they see the contradiction in our lives? Those are tough questions that only you can answer. Spiritual warfare can come in a variety of ways. Satan knows what strings to pull on each of us. You have to remain vigilant.

MARK 14:71 *But he began to curse and swear, "I do not know this man you are talking about!"*

169

DON'T GIVE UP

We know that as Peter spoke his third denial the night Jesus was taken away from the garden, a rooster crowed in fulfillment of Jesus' prophecy. Jesus knows the future because He is not bound by time, as we are. This reminds us that Jesus is sovereign. What does this have to do with Peter's failure and restoration in his spiritual battles? Not only did Jesus know ahead of time what Peter's responses were going to be, but Jesus also predicted that Peter would rebound from his breakdown and again become a leader among his fellow disciples (Luke 22:31–34).

In other words, Jesus was telling Peter that even though he would fail, his failure would not be terminal. Jesus was saying in effect, "Peter, I won't give up on you even after you deny Me and feel like a total failure." Jesus wanted Peter to remember this so he would not give up completely. His tears would then become tears of repentance and healing, not tears of despair.

Did you know that Jesus is praying for us too? If He were not, none of us knows how low we might go. If there's hope for Peter, there's hope for us. Peter's spiritual healing began at the most painful moment of his life, but it made him stronger than ever.

JOHN 17:24 *Father, I desire that they also, whom You have given Me, be with Me where I am, so that they may see My glory which You have given Me, for You loved Me before the foundation of the world.*

— 170 —

ROCK BOTTOM

It's obvious that even though Peter hit bottom in denying Christ, the other disciples didn't abandon him. They didn't kick him when he was down. So when Peter went fishing, many were with him. But if you read about it in John 21, you'll notice that they caught nothing. When you are out of the will of God, guess what you catch? Nothing. You cannot produce.

Peter had lost his vision for ministry. He was probably asking himself, "Can God still use me?" The answer was about to come when grace showed up the next morning in the person of Jesus Christ. Jesus answered Peter's question with the miraculous catch of fish. When you get right with God, you become productive again. When you get right with God, no matter how low you have gone, no matter far away you've strayed, things begin to happen again.

In Peter's life story, we see one of the greatest demonstrations of God's grace. Jesus restored Peter three times for his three denials. He invited him back into the fold, back into His service. Peter reaffirmed his devotion to Jesus, and Jesus gave him another chance. Peter was restored to fellowship with his Lord and recommissioned for his apostolic ministry.

JOHN 21:17 *He said to him the third time, "Simon, son of John, do you love Me?" Peter was grieved because He said to him the third time, "Do you love Me?" And he said to Him, "Lord, You know all things; You know that I love You." Jesus said to him, "Tend My sheep."*

—171—

SATAN'S MEAL PLAN

When Jesus taught us to pray, "Give us this day our daily bread," He was teaching us to depend on the Father as our source. But God isn't the only one offering us a meal plan. The devil wants to cook for us too.

Satan is often saying to us, "Since you are a child of God, I have a job for you. I have a way you can make money, get some bread, if you'll hook up with me and do things my way." But just as Jesus refused the devil's meal plan, so can you. Remember, "MAN SHALL NOT LIVE ON BREAD ALONE, BUT ON EVERY WORD THAT PROCEEDS OUT OF THE MOUTH OF GOD" (Matthew 4:4). What does that mean? It means you shouldn't only go for the bread. You should also be aware of the source providing it. Unless God is supplying it for you, steer clear of it. Always test the source.

Satan is a manipulator who can deceive you in many ways. He can even make you believe that what you are doing is good, or for God. So it is important to test the spirits. Test your beliefs against the Word of God, which reveals the truth. Never trade your spiritual wisdom or power for a piece of bread. What God has in store for you is of so much more value.

MATTHEW 4:4 *But He answered and said, "It is written, 'MAN SHALL NOT LIVE ON BREAD ALONE, BUT ON EVERY WORD THAT PROCEEDS OUT OF THE MOUTH OF GOD.'"*

—172—

RELIGION'S FAKE PEDESTALS

There's a huge difference between Christianity and religion. I touched on this earlier but want to revisit it as we start to wrap up our time together. If you get this issue wrong, you will not be equipped to fight any good fight at all. You will be easy pickings for Satan.

It is critical that you understand Christianity is about your relationship with and to Jesus Christ. The spiritual authority you have access to is rooted entirely in Jesus. It is not found in your own good deeds, your own righteousness, or your own good intentions. Spiritual authority comes because of Jesus Christ and His divine nature.

Religion focuses on what you do to earn God's favor, and allows people to think too highly of themselves. One of the things I'm discovering in filming the documentary *Unbound: The Bible's Journey Through History* is how fundamentally flawed a lot of the so-called great leaders in our Christian history were. We should not be surprised to learn this, nor should we be quick to judge them. It brings God glory when we see how He worked through flawed people to bring us the Word today in so many languages. As a result, rather than glorifying people, we can see who the true hero of this story is. Rules and religion will get us nowhere. It is only the grace of Jesus Christ that can accomplish through each of us what He chooses to do.

ROMANS 5:1 *Therefore, having been justified by faith, we have peace with God through our Lord Jesus Christ.*

—173—

RICH TOWARD GOD

If you want to be successful, it helps to have a vision. There was a successful farmer who built a big farm. In time, his business grew so much that he decided to build even bigger barns to handle all the stuff he was producing. This man's business was going up and up and up.

So he said he was going to retire. His 401(k) was working for him too. But when he chose to retire, heaven opened up and called him home. See, your bank account, your 401(k), and your barns can't help you when it's time to die.

The parable of the rich fool in Luke 12 is a reminder that we are to spend our time serving God rather than laying up for ourselves treasures and cash. When you accumulate wealth independently of God, putting God on the back shelf, God reminds you that He doesn't like to be put on the back shelf at all. It is foolish to live your life accumulating things and not be rich toward God. We've got a lot of people in our nation and the world who have money but are very poor spiritually because they are operating as foolish people toward God. A person who has made the physical more important than the spiritual will lose in spiritual warfare regularly. You must put God first in your heart and in allocating your resources in order to tap into His spiritual authority when you need it most.

PHILIPPIANS 4:20 *Now to our God and Father be the glory forever and ever. Amen.*

—174—

SHAKING THINGS UP

When your view of God gets bigger, your view of yourself gets smaller. That's exactly the way it should be. We have a society that seeks to elevate people for achievements. And that's not all bad. For example, you give honor to the policeman because of his role and his badge. You give honor to the judge because of his role and his robe. We honor others because of the extrinsic value their accomplishments have gained for them. But there is another kind of value. It's called intrinsic value. Another way to consider it is intrinsic glory. Intrinsic glory belongs to God simply because of who He is.

What wet is to water and blue is to sky, intrinsic glory is to God. You don't make water wet and you don't make the sky blue—it's just the way they are. Similarly, God is glorious because that's just how He is. He deserves all glory, praise, and worship. When He feels we have drifted from this understanding of Him, He sometimes allows things to get shaken up in our lives. He wants to reset things so we understand and know Him. He wants us to pursue our relationship with Him with passion. You are to prioritize His position in your life because He deserves to be the top priority. When you seek first His kingdom and His righteousness, then whatever you face coming at you from Satan will be handled in a way that brings Him glory and brings you good.

HEBREWS 12:29 *For our God is a consuming fire.*

—175—

FOLLOW ME

Making comparisons is great when you're shopping for the best deal. But comparisons can cripple your spiritual growth. Jesus had little patience for comparisons when He walked on earth. John 21:22 reveals one of His responses: "Jesus said to him, 'If I want him to remain until I come, what is that to you? You follow Me!'" We are not to concern ourselves with what other people do. We are to concern ourselves with what we are doing related to Jesus Christ. Are *you* following Jesus as His disciple?

Many of us can't get around to following Christ because we are too busy worrying about what other people are doing or what other people are achieving. Many of us blame someone else for our shortcomings as a disciple. But you cannot concern yourself with what other people do or say. Your discipleship is your responsibility.

What does that word *follow* mean? It means to come after. But it means to come after a person, not simply submit to a program. You can come to church without following Christ. You can listen to Christian podcasts and not follow Christ. You can have devotions every day and not follow Christ. This is because you've reduced it to a program and lost sight of the relationship. Jesus didn't say follow the program; He said, "Follow Me." No matter what's going on around you, follow Jesus. Abide in Him. As you do, you will gain strength to battle well.

MATTHEW 4:19 *And He said to them, "Follow Me, and I will make you fishers of men."*

—176—

CAFETERIA CHRISTIANITY

When you're following someone, you don't get to choose the route or the destination. If you do, it no longer qualifies as "following." That's true of what many Christ-followers do these days too, it seems. You must know something else about following Christ: It is a nonnegotiable trip. It's not like going to a cafeteria where you walk down the line to see all the options and choose what you want. In a cafeteria, you decide what you want along the way, saying no to some things and yes to others.

Following Christ is not like your local smorgasbord. It is not where you say, "Okay, Jesus, if You do that, I'll take that. I don't like this part of You, but I like that part of You." That's cafeteria Christianity, where you pick and choose the parts you want. Jesus Christ is not negotiating a relationship with you. He is telling you to follow Him. He's not asking you for directions either. Nor is He asking for your advice. Too many Christians want to negotiate their faith. They want to do what God wants done as long as what God wants done is what they want to do. But God is not negotiating. A victorious Christian who can overcome Satan's attacks is one who unreservedly follows Jesus Christ.

ROMANS 6:6 *Knowing this, that our old self was crucified with Him, in order that our body of sin might be done away with, so that we would no longer be slaves to sin.*

—177—

MILES TO GO

Christians who think they've arrived probably haven't. Pride is the first step down a long hill toward humility. Pride is one of the ways Satan trips people up. If the devil can get you thinking more of yourself than you ought, he's got you cornered.

One day when my kids were young, we were returning from California when we hit the Texas line. The sign said, "Welcome to Texas." The kids were excited to see that sign, and one of them yelled out, "Yay, we're almost home!" But we were nowhere near home. If you have ever driven across West Texas, you know what I mean. We had miles to go before we would reach the first town, and hours to go before we were home.

Spiritual growth can be tricky because you want to enjoy the moments when you grow and mature. But just because you are not where you used to be doesn't mean you still don't have a long way to go. Victories are great. Overcoming the enemy's strategies in your life is great. But there's so much further to go if you are going to follow Jesus Christ fully. He wants to take you to new heights and deeper depths in Him. So don't settle in when you gain some victories. Keep charging ahead.

1 CORINTHIANS 2:9 *But just as it is written, "THINGS WHICH EYE HAS NOT SEEN AND EAR HAS NOT HEARD, AND WHICH HAVE NOT ENTERED THE HEART OF MAN, ALL THAT GOD HAS PREPARED FOR THOSE WHO LOVE HIM."*

—178—

GRACE CAME DOWN

Many people think Christianity is all about people behaving better so they'll be more acceptable to God. But that's not only wrong, it's impossible. The good news of the cross is that God came down. The good news of Calvary is that God left heaven and came down to earth to lift us back up to heaven. That's grace. Wherever you see a gap between where you are and where Christ is, you don't need the power of positive thinking—you need grace to come down.

One of the great failures common today is Christians thinking they can fix whatever problem they are facing. Maybe they even promise to fix it, stop it, or change it. But even if they mean it, they don't have the power to apart from Jesus and His grace. Grace comes down and makes up the difference of what we lack in our humanity.

Now, God doesn't want us to sin, nor does He want us to fail. But when we do, and when we are restored, then we should become a minister of grace to others because we know what it's like to experience grace. We know what's it's like to wander down the wrong road. We know what it's like to be confused, humbled, and forgiven. This will often soften our hearts to be more compassionate toward others too. Receiving grace and giving grace enable us to walk in humility honoring God.

2 TIMOTHY 2:1 *You therefore, my son, be strong in the grace that is in Christ Jesus.*

—179—

CURING SELF-SUFFICIENCY

The biggest problem many people have following Jesus is the idea of following anyone at all. It's a disease called self-sufficiency. If you're going to follow Jesus Christ, I can guarantee you something: He will break you first. Accepting Jesus Christ is not all tiptoeing through the tulips. He is going to strip you of your self-sufficiency.

We have too many independent Christians who think they can overcome Satan's attacks all on their own. They do everything they can to make life work, but it doesn't—because God is opposed to pride. He might be trying to break you and strip you of your self-sufficiency.

Sure, it's painful to be told you don't know what you think you know. It's hard to follow Jesus sometimes when what Jesus says goes against what you think is right. Following Christ involves rejecting your feelings, rejecting your knowledge, and rejecting your experience, if Jesus says something different.

The reason God will break you is because He has something greater for you. He shows you that you don't know what you think you know, and that you aren't as strong as you think you are, so He can take you to places you've never been. Just as developing muscles hurts, spiritual growth and developing spiritual warfare muscles hurt as well. But it's worth it, so I encourage you to participate with the process even though you don't enjoy the pain.

ROMANS 11:6 *But if it is by grace, it is no longer on the basis of works, otherwise grace is no longer grace.*

—180—

ENLISTED FOR THE KINGDOM

Salvation is free, but it is not cheap. There is also a cost to discipleship. When a person joins the armed services, they join for free. You don't have to buy your way into the army or the navy. They will gladly receive you for free. But after they receive you, they're going to tell you what to wear, when to get up, and what to do. They're going to send you where they want you to go because even though you got in for free, they now own you.

Similarly, you can get saved for free. In fact, the Bible says you are saved apart from works (Romans 3:28). Jesus paid it all. You can't buy salvation. You can't earn salvation. You get it for free. But once you are saved, God wants to own your life. You are not your own; you have been bought with a price (1 Corinthians 6:19–20).

If God doesn't own you, even though you've been let in for free, then you're going to be in opposition to the Owner of the kingdom. This world has enough trouble of its own; you don't need to make any more for yourself. Honor God and seek Him first, and He will give you the strength and the wisdom to defeat the enemy and his attacks on your life, your loved ones, and all you care about.

EPHESIANS 6:1 *And take* THE HELMET OF SALVATION, *and the sword of the Spirit, which is the word of God.*

Honor God and seek Him first, and He will give you the strength and the wisdom to defeat the enemy and his attacks on your life, your loved ones, and all you care about.

DR. TONY EVANS is the founding pastor of Oak Cliff Bible Fellowship in Dallas, founder and president of The Urban Alternative, former chaplain of the Dallas Mavericks and the Dallas Cowboys, author of more than 150 books, booklets, and Bible studies. The first African American to earn a doctorate in theology from Dallas Theological Seminary, he has been named one of the 12 Most Effective Preachers in the English-Speaking World by Baylor University.

Dr. Evans also holds the honor of writing and publishing the first full-Bible commentary and study Bible by an African American.

His radio program, *The Alternative with Dr. Tony Evans*, broadcasts to millions of active listeners across hundreds of radio stations and digital outlets across the nation and around the world.

Dr. Evans launched the Tony Evans Training Center in 2017, an online learning platform providing quality seminary-style courses for a fraction of the cost to any person in any place. The TETC currently has over fifty courses to choose from and has a student population of over two thousand.

For more information, visit TonyEvans.org.

CONNECT WITH DR. EVANS:

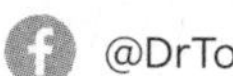

@DrTonyEvans

@DrTonyEvans

@DrTonyEvans